# SOCIAL ORGANIZATIONS

# SOCIAL ORGANIZATIONS

## Interaction inside, outside and between organizations

### GÖRAN AHRNE

## SAGE Publications
London • Thousand Oaks • New Delhi

SAGE Publications Ltd
6 Bonhill Street
London EC2A 4PU

SAGE Publications Inc
2455 Teller Road
Thousand Oaks, California 91320

SAGE Publications India Pvt Ltd
32, M-Block Market
Greater Kailash – I
New Delhi 110 048

**British Library Cataloguing in Publication data**

Ahrne, Göran
    Social Organizations: Interaction Inside,
    Outside and Between Organizations
    I. Title
    302.35

    ISBN 0–8039–8920–2
    ISBN 0–8039–8921–0 pbk

**Library of Congress catalog card number 94–66307**

Typeset by Photoprint, Torquay
Printed in Great Britain by Biddles Ltd, Guildford

# CONTENTS

# PREFACE

The key idea of this book is that what is going on inside, outside and between organizations is central in all analysis of society. Organizations are the mechanisms that shape macro-processes at the same time as they are the preconditions for everyday life.

Action and structure are brought together in organizations. Through organized interaction human actions are transformed into social processes. Organizations provide people with resources and motives and they set the frames for human action. Through organizations people acquire power, and their actions are reinforced through coordination with the actions of other people. Organizations are the most obvious components of society. They do not exist independently of conscious human activity, neither are they merely the product of such activities (see Bhaskar, 1989: 76).

I believe that the discussion in the 1980s about action and structure within social theory that has been labelled 'a new theoretical movement' (see Alexander, 1988) has been useful. It has brought different schools of thought closer to each other and paved the way for new syntheses. At the same time, however, much of this discussion has resulted in an abstract impasse (see Ahrne, 1990). The aspiration of an organizational approach to the discussion of action and structure is to propose an empirically relevant way out of this dilemma. But this approach would not have been possible without the previous theoretical insights.

The book begins with an investigation of the phenomenon of organization. The aim is to offer a real definition of organizations, that is, a definition that builds upon their basic nature (see Outhwaite, 1987: 45). A real definition of organizations includes statements and conclusions about how organizations shape human interaction in terms of, for instance, inclusion, exclusion and control.

The book follows the logic of this investigation. The discussion of other theories has been subordinated to the logic of my presentation. Other theories are discussed and cited when they are useful to support the arguments. In this process a substantial part of the literature on organizations as well as other literature has been covered. The method has been to join pieces of various theories together into a theoretical collage. Many topics that are raised would have merited a much more thorough penetration, but I have chosen not to break the general argument with such discussions.

In the first chapter the investigation starts from the assertion of four main features of human interaction that together make up the universal pattern of organization: affiliation, collective resources, substitutability of individuals and recorded control. Through their affiliation to particular organizations individuals get access to resources and power, but they are also controlled and they have to promise to come back.

Most human actions are actions on behalf of organizations. In chapter 2 I discuss the dual involvement of individuals in such actions. People acting on behalf of organizations can be regarded as organizational centaurs: part human and part organization. In chapter 3 I outline the organizational mechanisms that transform individual actions into social processes. In this chapter the development of the four main concrete types of organization in the world today – families, states, enterprises and voluntary associations – are described.

Not everything in society is organized. Outside organizations there are other forms of human interaction and there are other social phenomena. Institutions and networks can be understood as complementary to organizations, and in chapter 4 I discuss their characteristics. Much of the human interaction outside organizations takes place in semi-organized fields. They are also analysed in chapter 4.

Organization theory in general has more to contribute to the development of social theory than is usually assumed. My approach towards theories of organizations is pluralistic. It is an effort to make a partial synthesis of several directions within the field of organization theories (see Reed, 1992: 265–6). The aspiration is to go 'beyond paradigmatic closure in organizational enquiry' (Willmott, 1990). In terms of organization theory the suggested approach probably comes closest to what may be called a new and broader contingency theory of organizations that includes institutional, as well as ecological and economic approaches to the analysis of organizations. In the book there is no presentation of theoretical schools in themselves; instead pieces of theories have been used where they fit into the general logic. As a whole, the presentation in the book is meant to be more constructive than critical. In chapter 5 the traditional topic of organization theory, that is, what goes on inside organizations, is covered through a combination of old and new concepts and explanations.

The notion that organizations are the main components of society does not imply that society is organized. It is rather the opposite. Organizations do not form societies or systems, but society is shaped and changed through interaction between organizations. This is the topic of the final two chapters of the book. In chapter 6 a discussion of power in relation to organizations is central for understanding various modes of interaction between organizations, such as competition, conflict and cooperation. Negotiations are analysed as a transitory form of interaction that involves talking about power. The organizational approach to social analysis suggested here would be falsified if there were a social order, such as a system or a culture above the level of organizations that determined the occurrence and form of organizations in particular places. Instead, in chapter 7 it is demonstrated that differences between the same type of organization in different constellations can be attributed to time sequences in the spread of organizations. We also discuss how organizations move and the role of institutional processes for the spread of organizations. There is an increasing tendency towards a globalization of the interaction between organizations.

An organizational approach to the analysis of society cannot explain everything. In this book there is no discussion on changes of values and motives among individual actors. Ideologies and values are important for understanding which organizations people want to support or join, although they are probably not as important as many social theorists claim. Irrespective of values or motives, all evidence indicates that the organized forms for collective action tend to be the same. Forms of interaction in political parties are the same for conservatives, liberals and radicals alike.

During the writing of this book I have been working at several research institutes: the Swedish Collegium for Advanced Study in the Social Sciences (SCASSS) in Uppsala, the Department of Sociology, Uppsala University, the Institute of Political Economy, Carleton University, Ottawa, and the Department of Sociology, Stockholm University. The research that is reported in this book has also been made possible through a grant from the Swedish Council for Research in the Humanities and Social Sciences (HSFR). To all these organizations I express my gratitude for financial and collegial support.

Chapters and parts of the book have been discussed in seminars at these institutes as well as at meetings with the Scandinavian Sociological Association in Trondheim in 1991 and in Gävle in 1993, and at a meeting with the Swedish Sociological Association in Uppsala in 1992. Parts of the book have also been presented at conferences in Växjö on leadership and organization arranged by Jon Andersen and Bengt Abrahamsson, at the F-section (public management), Stockholm School of Economics, and at the Department of

Business Administration, Uppsala University. I wish to express my thanks for stimulating comments and criticisms received on these occasions.

Chapter 6 is written jointly with Roine Johansson and chapter 7 with Apostolis Papakostas, but their contributions to the book have been far greater than that. I owe them many thanks for ideas and inspiration. Special thanks for extensive comments and good advice are due to: Howard Aldrich, Thomas Coniavitis, Mats Franzén, Carl le Grand, Peter Hedström, Håkon Leiulfsrud, Rolf Lidskog, Per-Anders Lindén, Sven Ross, Kerstin Sahlin-Andersson, Richard Swedberg, Michael Tåhlin and Lars Udéhn.

# 1

# ORGANIZED INDIVIDUALS

## Why do you go home?

Everyday life is routine and repetitious. The coming and going of people in their everyday lives is far from arbitrary. People know where they are going and to where they have to return. Routines are patterned and organized. Nowadays, the two most important nodes of everyday life are the home and the job. After work people go home and next morning they go to their jobs again. Children go to school and come home again.

Many people like their jobs and also want to go home. And many children love to go to school. This is not enough, however, to explain the order of everyday life. If it relied merely on what people wanted to do, it would be rather chaotic. People go to their jobs, and children go to school and return home again even if they do not feel like it. Additional explanations could be the power of habits and norms, which certainly is important. Still, the answer to the mystery of the order of everyday life also has to be looked for in the organizational mechanisms of the nodal points.

First of all, people have commitments to come to their jobs and to come home at certain times. Children are usually obliged to attend school. This means that there are other people there who check on you, and they will be angry and chastise you if you do not turn up on time. And there are sanctions. After some time you may risk losing your job and your family if you do not keep your promises. There are others who may take your place. In their everyday lives people are very much aware of such preconditions.

Moreover, your home and your job are places where you have the right to enter, you are recognized and let in. You cannot go to any job or any home. In fact, there are not many places you can go to spend the day or the night. Furthermore, you need the income from your work and you need to go home to rest and sleep and to change clothes.

The power of attraction of the nodes of everyday life is generated through four conditions that characterize and determine forms of human interaction:

(a) affiliation
(b) collective resources
(c) substitutability of individuals
(d) recorded control.

A central argument will be that these nodal principles together constitute common features in basic social units such as families, enterprises, clubs or states. They are combinations of forces that make people part of social entities. We will call these entities organizations, a well-established term for some of them but not for all, although Chester Barnard (1968: 4–5), for instance, had no hesitation in regarding families as organizations.

The basic idea is that organizations in this sense are central to social analysis. The four features of organization constitute the most persistent and universal relations between individuals (see Bhaskar, 1989: 71), and organizations set the conditions for human action. Organizations are stronger and more persistent than either individuals or societies, and they constantly transcend borders of societies or systems. Organizations are the locus of the connection between individuals, and through them human actions are transformed into social processes. What has been discussed as the structuring of interaction (see Turner, 1988: 150) above all happens in the form of organization.

The relationship between individuals and organizations is

inherently ambivalent. Organizations do not want anything, nor do they have any will of their own or any purpose; only human agents have. Only human beings can act. On the other hand, human purposes and wants cannot easily be understood without relating them to the organizational affiliation of an actor. Organizations are social mechanisms that connect a large number of human wishes and hopes into common consolidated actions.

Organization is a link between human beings that unites some people, while separating them from others. This link is not established by individuals themselves but precedes their relationships and will probably exist after they have gone. Organizations are independent of particular individuals, but without individuals an organization would not exist.

The term 'organization' does not seem to be popular among social theorists. Many prefer concepts such as groups, movements, teams or collectivities. Organization is associated with bureaucracy and hierarchy. Still, we think organization is the most appropriate term for the kind of social entity that is the subject of this book, although used in an extended sense.

Organizations can be seen as probably the most important example of a 'figuration', which makes it possible to think 'of people as individuals at the same time as thinking of them as societies' (Elias, 1978: 129; cf. Ahrne, 1990). Barnard put it simply when he saw 'formal organization as the concrete social process by which social action is largely accomplished' (1968: 3). The aim is to make an investigation into the fundamental and common bonds that make organizations into the primary 'unified socio-individual field' (Sztompka, 1991: 94) comprising both individualities and totalities.

There are examples of approaches that emphasize the importance of organized interaction, although they do not mention organizations. In his book *The Presentation of Self in Everyday Life* (1959) Erving Goffman gives a description of 'teams'. For Goffman teams are 'any set of individuals who co-operate in staging a single routine' (1959: 79). The familiarity among teammates need not be organic, but rather 'a formal relationship that is automatically extended and received as soon as the individual takes a place on the team' (1959: 83). Teams must not be confused with informal groups or cliques. As examples of teams he mentions 'marriage teams', the staff of a tourist hotel and a factory. Thus, Goffman's discussion of teams lends support to our description of organizations, although Goffman's treatment is vague (see also Goffman, 1968: 159; cf. Burns, 1992: 376–7).

Another sociologist who writes about organizations without admitting it is Michael Hechter in his book *Principles of Group Solidarity* (1987), where he defines groups as: 'a collection of individuals who are engaged in a specific type of mutually oriented activity (or set of interconnected activities), entry to which occurs according to one or more criteria of membership' (1987: 16). The condition of membership criteria is important. In Hechter's book all examples in the four empirical chapters are from organizations such as political parties and large corporations. He also discusses families. We will return to Hechter's book later in this chapter and to Goffman in chapter 2.

Sometimes sociologists use the term 'institution' or 'the institutional order' more or less as a synonym with organization, but usually not to denote only organizations (see Gerth and Mills, 1970: 24; Giddens, 1984: 17). In organization theory the term institution has had a renewed currency in what is called 'the new institutionalism in organizational analysis'. In this approach institution represents 'a social order or pattern that has attained a certain state or property' (Jepperson, 1991: 145). Institutions are relative properties and depend on the purpose of the analysis. Thus they should not be specifically identified.

Generally, we will argue that it is essential to make a sharp distinction between institutions and organizations. Institutions are ideas about which social activities can be organized and how they should be organized. Thus, an institution is first of all a set of cultural rules that may regulate social activities in a patterned way (Meyer et al., 1987: 36). Organizations are materialized institutions. Every organization has a location and an address. Organizations have a quite different relation to human actors from institutions, and organizations have a more pronounced position in the ordering of everyday life.

## Affiliation, recognition and exclusion

In the beginning there is organization. The basic human experience is belonging and dependence. We will argue that affiliation to organizations is a prerequisite for most human action. Some organizational bonds are virtually impossible to break. The idea of kinship has survived the twentieth century. The importance of citizenship becomes increasingly obvious in a rapidly globalizing world. Solidarity between people seems to be limited without organizational bonds.

To belong to an organization means to have a place to go, to have certain rights as well as commitments. Affiliation implies a promise or an obligation to come back. To be able or allowed to come back, the affiliates of an organization have to be recognized or they have to prove their affiliation. To be recognized you need some kind of identification, be it a name or a number. If you are not recognized you will not be let in. This is a basic human experience with important and far-reaching consequences although it is often neglected because it is taken for granted (see Aldrich, 1979: 2).

Gates of organizations are locked and guarded. Only affiliates have a key, but not always all of the affiliates. Those who are not affiliated have no right to enter. If you are not recognized you are not let in. All organizations are exclusive (see Barnard, 1968: 149).

As an affiliate of an organization the other affiliates give you an identity, they begin to recognize you and they care about what you do, when you come and when you leave. They depend on you and count on you. You mean something. Outside organizations, in the semi-organized field, you are anonymous and nobody demands anything from you.

The social individuality is mainly a combination and construction of previous and present organizational affiliations: family background, citizenship, grades from school, previous and present employments, marital status (see Meyer, 1987b: 250). Belonging and affiliation are necessary for individuality. To be an individual you have to be recognized. When you lose your job or when you divorce you lose part of your identity.

This is not to say that organizations are inherently just and that affiliates are always taken care of and treated fairly. On the contrary, organizations are often repressive and terribly unjust. The affiliates of an organization have diverging interests. Yet, they generally have one interest in common, the survival of the organization.

The reality of organization is as old as mankind. The roots of affiliational bonds stem from the earliest forms of families and tribal relations. Cooperation and solidarity were indispensable for security and survival (see Keesing, 1975).

In the course of time many forms of affiliation have been invented and practised, such as slavery and serfdom. More recent and sophisticated forms of affiliation have grown up in later centuries, such as citizenship and employment. In the future new forms of affiliation may develop. The most striking fact, however, is that organizational affiliation as such has been the fundamental bond between people throughout. Cooperation between individuals is not a puzzle but a fact. The question to be asked is rather how is individual action possible, or at least when, and under what conditions?

In the social science literature the problem is often the reverse, perhaps not so much in sociology as in other disciplines. In their well-known book *The Social Construction of Reality*, Peter Berger and Thomas Luckmann (1967) describe the origin of institutions as a process that evolves from repeated interaction of a few individuals, which first becomes habitual and later is transformed, according to Berger and Luckmann, into an institution. Our argument, however, is that the process is the other way around; first comes affiliation then interaction, habits and routines. Generally, the organization is already there. When new organizations are created, as when a couple gets married or when people start a soccer club or a political party, the origin is generally institutional, which means that there are already rules and routines for how it all should take place. An entrepreneur already has an idea of how the organization should look.

One of the most important tasks in all organizations is to keep track of those who are affiliated with the organization. Each citizen, employee, owner, child, or member is carefully recorded and identified with a particular name or number or some other identification. The development of organization theory during the past years has caused the common misunderstanding that organizations are rather loose and nebulous entities. Concepts such as 'loose coupling' or 'garbage can decision processes' have contributed to this notion (see Powell, 1991: 189). The limited rationality of organizations is obvious, but still the boundary-maintaining activities in organizations are as important as ever. All organization implies that 'a distinction has been made between members and non-members – some persons are admitted to participate in the organization, whereas others are excluded' (Aldrich, 1979: 4; cf. Weber, 1968: 48). Forms of affiliation such as employment, citizenship or membership are decisive for such important organizational activities as paying wages, paying taxes or paying membership fees. The rules for marriages vary considerably in different parts of the world, but whatever the rules, independent of how many wives a husband may have, the family is always and everywhere strictly defined in terms of its actual members.

To become affiliated with an organization you are selected. It is not only your own choice. You can choose to apply for a certain job, or you can propose to get married, but the ultimate choice is not yours. You have to be admitted.

Affiliation cannot usually be bought. You cannot buy a job,

a citizenship or kinship. To become a member of a voluntary association it is, generally, not enough to pay the membership fee. You must be accepted, and you can be excluded if you do not satisfy certain requirements. Ownership, however, is, in principle, for sale in the stockmarket. But ownership of a minor amount of the shares in a big company is not a genuine form of affiliation, although it gives rights to take part in shareholders' meetings. Big powerful shareholders, however, do not sell their shares to anybody. They make special offers to those whom they want as owners, and there are various ways to control access to ownership rights. Thus, there is a moment for exclusion in ownership.

Affiliation implies a promise to come back. It is hardly meaningful to say that an affiliate chooses to return each time. Is it meaningful to say that you chose to go home after work or that you chose to go to your job this morning? The choices that make a difference are the decisions to join or leave an organization. Once someone has joined an organization the act of coming back is often rather a matter of routine.

Affiliates of an organization 'give up the right to control certain of their actions', as James Coleman (1990: 66) expressed it in his book *Foundations of Social Theory*. He denotes this as 'vesting of authority'. He also adds, however, that not all authority is the result of a voluntary vesting (1990: 72). This is the case in the family or in the state (1990: 67–8). Still, it seems that Coleman does not really take these restrictions of the right to control one's actions seriously, since his theory presupposes the assumption that individuals from the start have full control over their actions. For him the most fundamental question is how authority structures can exist at all (1990: 66).

There seems to be a prevailing notion in much of sociology and social sciences that with modernization ascribed status has been replaced by achieved status in determining human life-chances. The idea is that people in the modern world have greater possibilities to choose their own way of life irrespective of where they come from. This may be true to some extent, but it has been greatly overemphasized. Ascribed status is still of utmost importance. Much research has demonstrated the surviving importance of family background for education and class position. Even more overlooked, however, is the importance of ascribed citizenship. Citizenship determines to a large extent other living conditions and there are few possibilities of influencing or changing this status (see Walzer, 1983: 32). As long as citizenship determines where you can live, ascribed status dominates social life. The reason citizenship has been a neglected concept in sociology may be that sociological theory has been addressed to the analysis of separate societies (see Brubaker, 1992: 22). Thus the notion of citizenship is taken for granted. In a theory including the whole world, however, citizenship obviously becomes important.

Organizational affiliation can be either voluntary or compulsory (see Weber, 1968: 52–3; Gerth and Mills, 1970: 24–6). In states affiliation is compulsory. The only way to escape this form of affiliation is to get a citizenship in another state, which is a demanding procedure. As an organizational form the family is connected with kinship bonds. Kinship is compulsory and virtually impossible to escape. Marriage, on the other hand, is generally voluntary and in most parts of the world it is possible to get divorced. But nowhere are you allowed to denounce your children. Employment is a voluntary form of affiliation that can pertain to all kinds of organization. Generally, all affiliation to enterprises is voluntary as well as affiliation to voluntary associations such as parties, trade unions or sports clubs. Voluntary association, however, does not imply that all who want can become affiliates. Michael Walzer writes in a general discussion on 'membership': 'so long as members and strangers are, as they are at present, two distinct groups, admissions decisions have to be made, men and women taken in or refused' (1983: 34). Voluntary organizations, whether they be enterprises or voluntary associations, are generally strict about who is to be admitted as an affiliate, whereas organizations with compulsory membership cannot deny affiliation to those who are born into the organization. Organizations with compulsory affiliation also have few possibilities to get rid of their affiliates (one extreme way is killing them). In both enterprises and voluntary associations affiliates can be dismissed.

Everybody has at least two kinds of affiliation, kinship and citizenship. Most persons, though, have several other affiliations. In the course of their everyday lives people move between several organizational affiliations, which is different from social roles (see further chapter 2). It is a matter of real bonds between existing persons and particular organizations.

In their everyday lives people are connected to and cooperate with several different sets of other people in different organizations. There are people checking when they come home or come to the job and their performances are recorded at home, on the job or at school. In principle, these mechanisms are the same in all forms of organizing. From this perspective the distinction between public and private organizations becomes confusing and highly doubtful (see Pateman, 1989: 122–3). To us, the idea of a private organization seems to be contradictory. And many individuals may experience more privacy on the job than in the family. No organization is public in the sense that it is open to anybody – a state is certainly not; and no organization is private in the sense that it is not known to the outside world. All families are publicly announced and known.

Affiliation to an organization is a form of pledge (Sartre, 1976: 421). The pledge often takes the form of a ceremony or ritual. The best-known example is the wedding. In many states new citizens have to swear an oath (allegiance). This is not unusual in voluntary associations either. The baptism of a child is the symbol of giving an identity to a new affiliate. Different forms of initiation rites are also common (see Brown, 1988: 23–6).

New affiliates, generally, get a written document to present as a proof of their recognition – a marriage certificate, a passport, or a membership card. It can also be a contract.

Employment, for instance, is sometimes arranged through formal contracts. It must be remembered, though, that an organization is more than a bunch of contracts, although we believe that it is reasonable to understand organizations as a 'series of contract-like agreements' with specific rights and duties (Keeley, 1988: 16).

Typically affiliation to an organization is not limited in time. One does not get married or join a political party for only a year or two. Even if an organizational affiliation may not be expected to last forever, it is commonly assumed to last as long as possible, or at least into some unforeseeable future. In his discussion of the evolution of cooperation Robert Axelrod stresses the importance of the 'shadow of the future' (1984: 173). Cooperation emerges in situations where 'the interaction is likely to continue for a long time, and the players care enough about their future together' (1984: 182). There are exceptions, however. One example is professional football or ice-hockey players, who are bought and sold for limited amounts of time.

Many organizations are surrounded by a semi-organized field where admittance is allowed to anybody. Restaurants, supermarkets and theatres are examples of semi-organized fields, where people are let in without being recognized. Sometimes, of course, they have to pay to get in, but they do not have to promise to come back. (In chapter 4 we will describe the semi-organized field.) The real organizational gates of supermarkets and theatres are the staff entrances and the stage entrances, which are well guarded.

Organizational affiliation is also exclusive in the sense that, generally, people are allowed to become affiliated with only one of all organizations of the same kind. If you are affiliated with one you are denied affiliation in all others. This is the case with marriage, membership of political parties, religious affiliation, membership of football clubs as well as citizenship. There are a few exceptions. Some states allow double citizenship, but it is unusual. And certainly one cannot become a citizen of many states. Employment, however, is not as exclusive as these other forms of affiliation. Still, there are many restrictions on the possibilities of being employed in two competing enterprises, for instance. Then also, of course, time is finite.

Organizational gate-keeping and exclusion is one of the foremost mechanisms of social control. In the course of their daily lives people do not have many choices of where to go. When you are going home after work there is only one home where you will be let in. You cannot choose between different jobs each morning. Even if there are many mothers in the houses around the playground, each child has only one home.

## Collective resources and power

Why is organizational affiliation such a strong force? What is it that binds people together? It is not only the wish for company that makes people come back. Nor is it only that they have nowhere else to go.

The core of all organization is a set of collective resources that is produced, maintained and used by the affiliates of the organization. The reason affiliates come back is that they have some interest in these resources, they need them and want them. They can also be forced to contribute to the maintenance and production of these resources. When people hesitate to leave an organization it is often because they have invested work, money or time into the production and maintenance of the resources of the organization, investments that are not easy to take with you if you leave since they belong to the organization. The fewer common resources in an organization, the more likely it is to be dissolved (see chapter 5).

Organizations are frequently associated with and located in buildings, which sometimes become their symbols: a home, a temple, a church, a factory, an office building, a supermarket, a school, a hospital, the party headquarters. The building itself with its equipment or technology is often the main resource of the organization. The architectural structure reveals a good deal about the structure of the organization.

Often the building is connected with a piece of terrain such as a garden or a golf course. Even if a family does not own the house they are living in they probably own some furniture, and perhaps they have some heirlooms from parents or grandparents that are common resources of the family members. Even if the organization does not have a building of its own it usually has some other form of common property such as money funds or equipment that it maintains and uses.

The resources and property of an organization make it into something more than the sum of its affiliates. Resources give continuity to the organization, and the persistence of a specific organization can be traced and defined according to its property.

In all organizations there are rules for the redistribution of resources, which, however, is rarely fair and equal. In most organizations there is an ongoing struggle about how to distribute resources such as wages, social benefits, pocket money. There are also rules and practices for how resources and properties should be transferred to new affiliates and new generations.

The importance of understanding the phenomenon of organizations in relation to their resources has been stressed by several researchers but rarely in a general way. McCarthy and Zald (1987a: 18) have emphasized the role of resources in connection with social movement organizations (cf. Knoke and Prensky, 1984). McCarthy and Zald also make clear that resource aggregation 'requires some minimal form of organization'. Possible access to some resources can often be seen as a cause of the creation of a new organization.

There are different kinds of resources, and some resources are more easily connected with organizations than others. Economists and rational choice theorists discuss resources, or joint goods, in terms of their 'publicness'; resources can vary from total publicness to total privateness. The degree of publicness or privateness of the resources is determined by the possibilities to exclude people from access to the utility or use of the good in question (see Hechter, 1987: 33–7). It is impossible to exclude anybody from the use of totally public goods. For private goods it is just the opposite. They are owned, controlled and used by only one person, that is to say, privately. Now, the point is that most resources are neither totally public (Hardin, 1982: 18–19) nor totally private. Most goods are collective or quasi-public with varying amounts of excludability. 'To the degree that collective goods are excludable, they can be produced for the sole consumption of members' (Hechter, 1987: 36).

When we do not confine our analysis to a particular 'society', it becomes obvious that few joint goods are completely public; what are regarded as public goods are generally confined to citizens of one particular state. The military defence of a state is not a public good, at least not for the enemies. When it comes to private goods, only simpler and cheaper consumable goods such as clothes or cigarettes are really privately owned and consumed. In fact, most goods or resources such as buildings, furniture, cars, all kinds of machinery, art etc. are collective or quasi-public goods and thus owned and controlled by organizations, that is, collectively owned. It is only a small share of all property that is owned by single individuals. It is the need and wish for all these collective goods, things one cannot get and keep on one's own, that make people join organizations and also promise to come back.

One important reason why people come back can thus be assumed to be their interest in getting access to things and activities that they would not otherwise be able to get. These may be things they cannot afford to buy, or do not have the time to maintain themselves, or just cannot do by themselves; things that are neither public nor completely private, that is, collective goods.

Resources or goods cannot only be classified according to whether they are public, quasi-public or private. Resources can also be more or less interchangeable or replaceable. To be in need of or want things that are difficult to replace creates a greater uncertainty. In order to secure the supply of and access to such things people can organize themselves around the protection, production or maintenance of them. To be dependent on something that is difficult to replace increases the dependence on the organization (Hechter, 1987: 45–8).

The possibilities of obtaining things that are difficult to replace can be analysed in terms of transaction costs. In Oliver Williamson's analysis, transaction costs are related to asset specificity which denotes 'idiosyncratic attributes of transactions' (Williamson, 1985: 53). Williamson distinguishes between four types of asset specificity: 'site specificity, physical asset specificity, human asset specificity and dedicated assets' (1985: 55). From the point of view of the affiliates of an organization, this means that to make the organization stronger and more efficient they want to secure the supply of assets that are of particular importance for their activities, such as certain goods, or raw material, or certain people with special skills or ideas, items that are costly to replace.

In order to explain the nature of organizing, the notion of asset specificity can be used also outside an economic context. Several voluntary organizations, such as professional organizations and trade unions or even political parties, can be understood as efforts to secure the 'supply' of members with certain skills, professions, or political convictions in order to mobilize them for certain purposes. Even marriage may be understood in these terms. Love and affection create human asset specificity.

Furthermore, resources are connected with power. Some resources, such as weapons, are more than others kept and produced in order to secure a position of power. All resources, though, may in particular circumstances become power resources. As an affiliate of an organization you get access to certain power resources that you can make use of. Resources of many kinds can give power: weapons, money, knowledge, status etc. The power of a politician depends on the resources of his or her party and in international relations on the resources of the state. The power of a businessman depends on the power resources of the company he works for. We will argue that to understand the use of power in social life, we should first of all relate power to organizations (see Clegg, 1989: 17; Latour, 1986: 276). The relations of power involved in human interaction almost invariably stem from the organizational affiliation of the actors involved (see further chapters 2 and 6).

Organizational affiliation gives rights to the use of resources, but it also implies obligations to contribute to the production and maintenance of them through membership fees, taxes or through labour. These rights and obligations are generally regulated beforehand, but they are not equally shared among all affiliates. Non-affiliates, though, are excluded from access to the resources of the organization – 'members only', 'private property'.

Not all resources, however, are reserved for members or affiliates. Such resources are for sale, as in shops or supermarkets. Or people can buy tickets to see a play at the theatre or to travel by a train. This is the semi-organized field, where affiliation is not a requirement for entry. In the semi-organized field there are also intermediate forms that come rather close to organizing, but which are not full organizations, such as the Book of the Month Club. Even though the 'members' in such an organization have certain commitments one cannot regard them as affiliates, since they have hardly yielded any authority over the right to control their own actions.

In many discussions of collective action the problem of human cooperation seems to be a mystery. The merit of this approach is to draw attention to the fact that all human interaction is not organized. Even though organization and cooperation is the basis for human action, everything or anything cannot be organized. Also failures to organize or failure of collective action should be understood and explained (see Hardin, 1982: 5). Generally though, our intuition is that a failure of collective action or organization is seldom due to a lack of cooperation altogether. The failure of one organization to recruit members is generally not due to the failure of collective action but to the success or power of another organization. Employers, for instance, have often been successful in preventing employees from joining or starting trade unions. A major obstacle to creating new organizations, that is, new forms of collective action, is an old organization, and there is always 'much more collective action in the world than a narrowly economic theory leads us to expect' (Udéhn, 1993: 257).

It is odd, however, to note in the literature on collective action the absence of the idea and reality of organization. Jon Elster, for instance, when discussing five main forms of cooperation does not mention organization as such (1989: 11–15).

Most definitions of organizations include a notion of goals. Organizations are seen as goal-directed (see Scott, 1992: 285–6). The idea of goals has been severely criticized, however (see for instance Perrow, 1978; Keeley, 1988: 46). One solution to the problem of organizational goals is to state that there are multiple or even contradictory goals in most organizations (Aldrich, 1979: 4). The notion of resources may be a better way to approach the problem of organizational goals. Goals are inscribed into the resources of the organization. Existing resources indicate the possible goals. Alternative uses of resources can account for changing or multiple goals, but any activity of an organization has to rely on its resources, which can be of various types such as technology, knowledge, money (capital), employees etc. Organizational resources account for the range of that organization's activities.

The motives for people to join an organization are also related to resources. Generally, it can be assumed that an important motive for joining an organization is the interest in getting access to or contributing to its resources. People with different political motives and values join different parties, but the parties are organized in the same manner.

Motives of affiliates of the same organization may vary even more than goals (Knoke, 1988: 326–7; Udéhn, 1993: 251). Sometimes motives are only indirectly related to resources. Some members may join a political party because they think other members are nice people. Yet, they will have to contribute to the production and maintenance of the resources of the party and pay attention to its main activities.

Resources also vary in terms of their mobility, that is, whether it is possible to move them around, to find new premises for example. Capital is a highly mobile resource that makes the mobility of enterprises rather high. The mobility of states, on the other hand, is very limited, since one of its resources, its territory, is hardly movable at all. Varying grades of mobility is one factor that explains strategies and power resources of organizations. This underlines the importance of relating organizations to their resources.

## Substitutability and the social reality of organizations

The recognition and identification of individual affiliates is indispensable for the running of an organization. Still, for the organization to last and survive no affiliate can be indispensable (see Selznick, 1948: 25). This is the paradox of organization. Even the most charismatic of leaders, even the most popular player must eventually be replaced if the organization is to survive. This constitutes a real problem for all organizations. Organizations both presuppose and transcend individual actors. The mystery is that the resources and goals of affiliates are both individual and organizational at the same time.

Probably, in most organizations, none of the present affiliates has experienced the foundation or beginning of that organization. They joined the organization or were born into it after it was settled. Their knowledge about how it all started is usually limited. They may have seen a picture of the founder on a wall in the main building, but that is all.

Resources and rules are transferred from old to new affiliates, who get access to resources that are already collected. In return they have to follow old rules. The resources of the organization, its buildings, machinery, capital, weapons, whatever, constitute the body of the organization while rules constitute its memory (Perrow, 1986: 26). The human affiliates give it life.

There are two aspects of the problem of substitutability. One can be seen as the problem of substitution and the other as the problem of succession. The problem of substitution concerns the day-to-day activities of the organization. Workers or football players can become ill or injured. For the organization to secure its activities requires the possibility of replacing affiliates that cannot do their tasks. There must be substitutes or reserves. Without substitutes the organization becomes vulnerable. For substitutes to be able to take their positions there must be rules or some other form of common knowledge about what to do (see Coleman, 1990: 427).

There are many ways to achieve succession. It can be inherited or successors can be bought from other organizations. Successors can be recruited from inside or outside the organization. They can be appointed by the person they will succeed or they can be elected by all the affiliates in various ways. In all organizations, however, the appointment of successors is a crucial problem that has to be solved if the organization is not to fall apart.

One of the most common methods to facilitate succession is the notion of career. The career in an organization is the ideal way to dissolve the contradiction between organizational unity and division. In a career the unity of the organization is learnt through the experience of several of its different positions.

The rules and the constitution of the organization make exchangeability possible, and together with the resources they make the organization into a social entity that exists independently of particular individuals. Organization is a combination of unity and division; there is no organization without some unity but there is also no organization without some division of labour or tasks. Rules pertain to both unity and division.

In the literature on theories of organizations the social reality of organizations is generally discussed under the title of organizational structure (Aldrich, 1979; Mintzberg, 1979; Perrow, 1986; Scott, 1992). In the notion of organizational structure are generally included such phenomena as hierarchy, bureaucracy, division of labour, rules, authority. Much emphasis has also been put on the existence of an informal structure in organizations. There are many variations in the form of organizational structure and much research has been done to explain different structural forms and also to find out what forms are most efficient or most democratic.

The important point here is the existence of an organizational reality which puts affiliates into positions and provides them with resources to do certain tasks they would not otherwise do nor would be able to do. Positions are independent of individuals. This is not to say that everybody can do anything in all organizations. For all positions, though, there must always be at least some other people who can act as substitutes or successors. Otherwise the organization is in real danger (for further discussion see chapter 5).

Human characteristics do matter, however – basic qualities such as sex or age, for instance. Enterprises may need people with a certain education and experience. A soccer club may need a special kind of player with certain abilities. A state, however, cannot choose its citizens. They have to be educated, and families have to bring up their own children. Some organizations, generally voluntary organizations, have youth organizations to try to secure the recruitment of new affiliates. Enterprises can take apprentices. To secure the supply of good substitutes or successors is a problem and a necessity for all organizations.

The structure of the organization presupposes both division and unity. In the literature on organizations the notion of unity is often expressed in terms of organizational culture or ideology.

In the organization an ideological consistency is upheld, which means that 'members are induced to think similarly and to recognize their ideological similarities' (Brunsson, 1985: 149). Brunsson also talks about a unitarian culture in organizations. Elements of an organizational culture can be rites and ceremonies, symbols as well as organizational 'sagas' (Ouchi and Wilkins, 1985; for further discussion see chapter 5).

Organizations celebrate anniversaries and there are rites for the introduction of new affiliates or for affiliates who are leaving the organization. Practically all organizations have a symbol of some kind or some colours. The symbol is reproduced above the entrance gate, on flags and banners, on products and on uniforms or other garments such as hats or T-shirts. Nationalism can be comprehended as an organizational culture for the state with the same function and expression. States have symbols, ceremonies, rites and sagas just like other organizations. Families also can easily be seen to display the same forms of organizational culture and ideology. The notion of its own uniqueness is a universal feature in all organizations.

The need for an organizational culture varies with type of organization. And it is far from certain that all affiliates embrace the organizational culture to the same extent. Some may actively oppose it.

Yet, the culture of an organization facilitates the substitutability of affiliates. It helps to introduce new affiliates and it gives a way of referring to the organization in contrast to all other organizations. The culture of an organization strictly adheres to the organization and not to individuals.

## Recorded control

People depend on organizations and spend most of their time in the realms of organizations. Most of their actions are motivated by organizational affiliations and commitments. Yet, people resist being organized and often refuse compliance. People do not become easily fused with their positions in the organizational structure.

Despite their promises to come back, despite their interests in the resources of an organization, despite ideological and cultural pressures, people try to escape the pressure of being organized. Michael Hechter makes the assumption that people will invariably prefer to pursue their individual ends before collective ends if they have a choice (1987: 41). One does not have to be as cynical as theorists influenced by the rational choice tradition, however, to realize that affiliates often try to get away. To understand the necessity of control in all organizations suffice it to say that people often or sometimes deviate from their positions in the organizational structure. Now and then, they are lazy, tired, or angry. Even the risk or the suspicion that affiliates will not always do what they should or what they promised is enough to state that control is a necessary part of all organization.

Control is not the same thing as the structure of the organization, although part of the routines of control may be built into this structure (see Ouchi, 1977). First, it is the behaviour of each individual affiliate that has to be controlled. A prerequisite for control is that every affiliate has a unique identity and that relevant performances can be watched, registered and recorded. The aim of control is not only to stop individuals from doing things they are not allowed to do. It is also to know what they do, how well they do it, how much they do, how fast they do it, if they are improving their performances etc. Recorded control means that the records of each affiliate are kept and saved for longer periods of time. Accomplishments are added and compared.

Control takes time and is costly. And it is contested. Of course, it would be nicer and cheaper if affiliates could be trusted. Still, even ideological effects of the organizational culture have to be checked. Some form of control will always be necessary, although too much control will be inefficient and counterproductive.

Control is generally thought of as coming from above, from managers, supervisors, leaders, teachers, trainers, coaches, parents. It is probably true that control in most organizations comes from the top. Yet, it is wrong to understand the origin and existence of control as synonymous with hierarchy. We will argue that the origin of control is a necessary and spontaneous phenomenon in any organization irrespective of its particular structure. There is control in small organizations based on equality as well as in large hierarchical organizations.

Affiliates have conceded that they will comply with the wishes and demands of other affiliates in certain matters within a 'zone of indifference' (Barnard, 1968: 167–9). The range of the concession varies. Still, they have accepted that they must make some contribution to the activities and resources of the organization, but they cannot decide upon the size and nature of their input themselves. It can be in the form of money, labour, or other activities. To make their contribution more than once, however, every affiliate wants to be sure that the others make their contributions too. If someone suspects that other affiliates are cheating, he or she will probably hesitate.

To make people contribute in the long run it is necessary to be able to convince them that all members do what they promised. This is also the case in spontaneous organizations. Not even a member of a new protest organization wants to continue to distribute leaflets if he or she discovers that other members throw them away. In a state the willingness to pay taxes decreases if people suspect that others have the possibility of evading their dues. Therefore control is necessary in order to secure the delivery of resources. Affiliates who have made their contributions and kept their promises want to be controlled in order to demonstrate the necessity of control.

Michael Hechter has emphasized the role of formal controls. He distinguishes between the monitoring and sanctioning capacities of all forms of organization. 'A group's monitoring capacity depends on the degree to which it possesses information about individual compliance with corporate rules or obligations, and its sanctioning capacity on its ability to generate and dispense resources that discourage noncompliance' (1987: 59). It follows from agreement on the necessity of control inside organizations that things that cannot be controlled satisfactorily cannot be organized. Presence is easy to control, whereas thoughts are harder. Hechter has outlined a series of arrangements that are used to facilitate control. Visibility can be increased through architecture or through creating public rituals, for instance (1987: 163; cf. Foucault, 1975). Often rituals are used as a substitute for controlling thoughts.

Regarding organizational sanctioning it has been a truth taken for granted that the state has a 'monopoly of the legitimate use of physical force in the enforcement of its order' (Weber, 1968: 54). Yet, and this was hinted at by Weber (1968: 56), physical force is used within the family too; between husbands and wives and between parents and children. Even if parents generally do not beat their children they still have the right to hold their children and prevent them from doing things by force, even to lock them up at night. It seems that compulsory affiliation goes with the use of physical force or at least harsher means of control. In voluntary associations the ultimate sanction is to expel affiliates.

In organizations affiliates are not only controlled in order to prevent them from doing things they are not allowed to do; sanctioning is not only punishment. It is just as important to reward good performance as to punish bad performance. Here is a distinctive difference between control inside organizations that is directed towards affiliates and control of people in the semi-organized field such as customers, passengers, spectators. The organizational control is accumulative and directed towards the performance of each individual over a long period of time. In organizations there are records of individual performances at work, training, presence at meetings, grades in school. In the family parents watch over the performances of their children and spouses keep track of each other's conduct and achievements. When affiliates have good records they are rewarded in some form, such as money, sweets, promotion, a medal. If you have done your job well it feels good to be checked up on.

Outside organizations, in the semi-organized field, control is neither directed at individuals nor recorded in the same sense. Here control is used to prevent people from doing things they are not allowed to do, or to make people pay for goods or tickets. A good performance in the semi-organized field is not rewarded. You are not rewarded for obeying the laws and not stealing in the supermarket or keeping the speed limits on the road.

## Concluding discussion

The four main topics discussed in this chapter, affiliation, collective resources, substitutability and control, are features that characterize crucial aspects of interaction and dependence between two or more people.

Affiliation is a relationship where a number of people are included and recognized and have promised to come back, while others are excluded. In organizations affiliation usually stretches over an undetermined period of time, and it involves commitments to contribute to the activities of the organization. Non-affiliates are excluded. Affiliation is the single most decisive feature of the figuration of organization.

Many human relations are mediated via resources. Relations to resources denote relations to other people. The nature of this relationship to a large extent depends on qualities of the resource. Resources that can be characterized as quasi-public goods or by asset specificity are generally owned collectively, that is, through organizations.

Substitutability means that the nature of a relationship is not dependent upon any particular person. The relation can be repeated with other partners. No individual in the relationship may have unique knowledge or unique qualities that prevent cooperation without him or her.

Control means that some people watch and register the actions and performances of one or several other people during a period of time. In organizations control implies authority. Affiliates have conceded to being controlled.

People may be affiliated to a group without being organized, however, for example a group of tourists travelling in a coach through Europe, or a group of people that regularly eat dinner at each other's houses. A detective following and watching a person for a week or a month is certainly controlling him or her in some sense, but he does not have any authority over that person.

Much social interaction is characterizd by substitutability; the relationship between a taxi-driver and his passenger for instance, or two people sitting on a bench in a park. Substitutability, on its own, does not make an organization.

Interaction characterized by only one of these features does not constitute an organization, nor does a combination of two or three of them. All four are required. It is their very combination that makes the pattern of interaction into an organization. This pattern seems to be reproduced and repeated in new types and forms of organization. The form of affiliation varies, but its basic implications are the same.

It is complicated, however, to handle these four features one by one or in combinations of two or three, that is, combinations that do not constitute an organization. The concepts as such are not unambiguous enough. The meaning of each feature may vary slightly depending on what combination it is part of. If affiliation is said to exist outside the organizational context, for example in a group of tourists on a tour, it means a somewhat weaker use of the concept of affiliation, since it is clearly delimited in time and thus implies a looser form of commitment. It is a limited affiliation and it does not entail that one has consented to control in the sense that happens in organizations. In the combination of features some qualities may be enhanced.

If the combination of affiliation and control in the strict sense of the term is hardly conceivable outside organizations, why not describe organizations in terms of affiliation and control? To explain the rationale behind affiliation as well as control we believe it is necessary to emphasize collective resources as the basis for all organization. The need to regulate access to resources is the origin of both affiliation and control. This does not imply that the distribution of resources within an organization generally is just or fair. It means, however, that all forms of organizational affiliation entail a relation to a specific set of resources.

Moreover, the description needs to be completed by the fact that all affiliates of an organization are, in principle, substitutable. Despite the strong interdependence of affiliates in an organization no individual affiliate must be indispensable. In order to talk about an organization this substitution does not have to take place, but the possibility to exchange affiliates must exist. This possibility is manifested in rules, work tasks or a constitution. Affiliates must share a common knowledge of the activities of the organization.

Together, the four features discussed here constitute a certain pattern of human interaction with a remarkable stability and universality. One discovers the same pattern in families, in states, in voluntary associations as well as in enterprises. In this chapter it has been our aim to discuss similarities among all types of organization as nodes of human interaction. In chapter 3 we will deal with differences between types of organization.

There are other terms for denoting social entities sometimes mentioned together with, for instance, families and voluntary associations. One example is the concept of neighbourhood, which is, however, a different phenomenon. Neighbours are substitutable and they may be said to share some common resources, but people do not belong to a neighbourhood in the same sense as they are affiliated with an organization. One seldom clearly knows where the neighbourhood ends. At least the border is arbitrary, which it is not in an organization. Moreover, belonging to a neighbourhood is not exclusive in the same sense as being affiliated to an organization. Michael Walzer (1983: 36) emphasizes this distinction, and says that new neighbours can be welcomed or not, but 'they cannot be admitted or excluded'.

# 2

# ORGANIZATIONAL CENTAURS

## Acting on behalf of organizations

When we talk or write about organizations it is all too easy to use a language that describes organizations as actors. We say that a political party expresses its views, a car factory produces cars, a theatre stages a drama, a state declares war etc. Yet in the true sense of the term only human beings have the ability to act. It is easier to say that the organization makes a statement than to say that these individuals representing this organization made a statement that was decided by a majority of its board. In order to understand what happens in and around organizations, however, it is misleading to regard organizations as actors.

In organizations there are resources and rules. But organizations cannot speak or move; they have no legs to walk with, and no eyes to see with. When organizations do something it is always individuals who act. They do not act on their own account, but on behalf of the organization.

All affiliates of an organization act both on behalf of the organization and on their own. Everything that is done in organizations is enacted through the bodies of its individual affiliates. The organizational centaur is the embodiment of both actions on behalf of organizations and actions on behalf of the natural person; it is part organization, part human.

When individuals act on behalf of organizations they act as

part of the organization, but since they are humans they invariably supersede the organizational context. The organization supplies the actor with resources, tasks, goals, motives, knowledge etc., while the individual contributes muscles, brain, eyes and voice, a face and a body. An organization 'is made up of persons, but not of whole persons; each one enters into it with a trained and specialized part of himself' (Cooley, 1914: 319; cf. Barnard, 1968: 16–17; Keeley, 1988: 231; Coleman, 1990: 543).

Erving Goffman has penetrated into the relations between individuals and organizations. Although he is not clear in his writings about the concept of organization as such (see chapter 1; Burns, 1992), he has made important contributions to the understanding of what he describes as 'dual involvement' (1959: 169). In his book *Asylums* he expresses this predicament in the following way: 'Our sense of being a person can come from being drawn into a wider social unit; our sense of selfhood can arise through the little ways in which we resist the pull' (1968: 280).

When individuals act on behalf of organizations, which they often do, they also to some extent perform a personal act. The first kind of actions Goffman calls 'expressions given' and the second kind 'expressions given off'. Expressions given pertain to actions on behalf of the organization such as the job a waiter or a policeman has to do. Expressions given off, on the other hand, pertain to personal traits and feelings of the actor. They 'involve a wide range of action that others can treat as symptomatic of the actor, the expectation being that the action was performed for reasons other than the information conveyed in this way' (1959: 2).

As far as policemen are concerned, 'expressions given off' may consist in letting off lightly a person who has committed a minor offence; or it may be a case of taking bribes or of maltreating a particular person because he or she is a foreigner. A waiter who is personally acquainted with a guest may act differently towards him than to an unknown customer.

Many of the examples that Goffman give in *The Presentation of Self in Everyday Life* are from service occupations or occupations such as teachers and doctors. Their jobs, that is, their organizational affiliations, can be regarded, according to Goffman, as interaction constraints, which transform the activities of an individual into performances.

In later works Goffman called expressions given off either secondary adjustments (1968: 172) or role distance (1972; cf. Burns, 1992: 137). With the concept of role distance it will be possible to deal with 'the divergence between obligation and actual performance' (1972: 102). This is a way of describing the action of organizational centaurs and the fact that a dual involvement is always there when we try to understand organizational action. Individuals do things, but often not wholeheartedly; they even do things that they do not believe in. They do it routinely on behalf of an organization while their minds are on something else.

People may act on behalf of organizations and believe that what they do is the best and most rewarding task there is. Yet, they may feel the need to express a role distance. An example is the recently converted person who has joined a political party or church and distributes pamphlets in the street for the cause. When he meets an old friend, his boss, or a teacher, his behaviour changes. He may feel the need to say something disarming or apologetic.

When individuals act on behalf of organizations they only to a limited extent decide themselves what to do. Thus, when acting on behalf of an organization you cannot change your mind on your own, at least not on major issues. You have to refer to others, and it is far from certain that they will accept your proposed changes. This is a major strain in acting on behalf of organizations and accounts for the tension between obligation and actual performance.

The ideal image of human interaction is a dialogue of two persons who listen to each other, react on what they hear and modify their behaviour accordingly. This is an unusual situation. People have their hang-ups and ties. Spontaneous reactions are rare. There are always the others, **your** affiliates, who have to have their say and are easy to **blame**.

In interaction on behalf of organizations people interact face to face and talk to each other, but there is no directness in the relation since people cannot change their minds immediately in response to the other person (see R. Johansson, 1992). Reactions are conditional; they have to follow a rule or be approved by the organization – by a boss, other members, a spouse, parents, etc. Moreover, the same individual is probably affiliated with several organizations. Other affiliations and loyalties create tensions in actions on behalf of organizations. Relations to relatives may override loyalty to an employer, generating nepotism.

Our argument is that interaction on behalf of organizations is the most common form of human interaction when we regard a family as an organization. Affiliation to a family, i.e. being married or being a child, gives the same kinds of constraint on interaction as being employed in a shop or being a representative of a political party. Goffman made this point many times (see for instance 1959: 78–9).

There are three forms of interaction between organizational centaurs: (1) interaction between individuals within the same organization, for instance interaction between a supervisor and his or her subordinates; (2) interaction between individuals representing different organizations in, for instance, business negotiations, wars and soccer games; and (3) interaction that takes place outside the immediate realm of an organization, but where different organizational affiliations of individuals interacting considerably affect their interaction.

(1) Inside organizations interaction between individuals depends upon their position in the organization. Individuals are given resources and authority according to the division of labour in the organization. In this respect the interaction is predetermined by the organizational setting. Now, all research experience from inside organizations has shown that formal aspects are not enough. Informal, personal and bodily attributes and characteristics are essential in many situations. Certain people, perhaps of the same age or sex,

may find it easier to talk to each other and understand each other. Individuals in the same position interact out of the organizational context creating their own interaction patterns (see Lysgaard, 1961; Burawoy, 1979). Yet, organizational motives and resources always play a role. The point is that it is mixed. Even though personal qualities and characteristics are important, there are always constraints on interaction between people due to their respective positions in the organization.

(2) In interaction between individuals representing two different organizations this is even more obvious. Moreover, in such situations it becomes clear that the concept of role is not enough to cover the importance of specific organizational positions and affiliations. Two businessmen from different companies or two politicians from different parties, for instance, have the same roles, but the content of these roles cannot explain their interaction. It is first of all determined by the power resources and activities of each company or party. The outcome of the interaction is also conditional on their positions, that is, their authority to make decisions.

Apart from different organizational affiliations and resources, there are personal qualities that can influence the interaction between two indidivuals from different organizations. Conditions such as types of personality, if they know each other from previous occasions, if they come from the same geographical region, if they have common acquaintances etc., can be decisive for the outcome of the interaction. Interaction between organizational centaurs depends both on their organizational bonds and on their personal traits, and it is often hard to distinguish between them.

Clearly, interaction of this type cannot be comprehended only in terms of roles. It is necessary to take the organizational context of roles into account. It is the specific organizational affiliation and concomitant resources and goals that matter in interaction between representatives from different organizations. Inside organizations roles are turned into positions with specific tasks and resources. Affiliation implies a position for each affiliate within the organization.

Paul DiMaggio has pointed out the neglect of the concept of organization in most efforts to treat relations between 'micro' and 'macro' in social theories (1991: 78). DiMaggio connects organizations with roles, and he also writes about resources and control. However, he does not draw the full conclusions of the relationship between organizations and roles. The relationship between general roles such as businessman or politician and actual organizational positions is the same as that between institutions and organizations. Just as organizations are realized or materialized institutions (the idea of family as compared to an actual family), organizational affiliation and positions are realizations of roles. Institutions and roles give general ideas and knowledge about how to do things whereas organizations and positions supply the materializations and embodiments as well as the resources.

(3) The importance of organizational affiliation and particular organizational resources stretches outside the immediate organizational context. When people meet and mix in semi-organized fields such as cocktail parties, restaurants and bars, people often ask about the organizational affiliations of other people. If you know that a person is employed by a certain company or university your interaction with this person is affected. A person's position and behaviour to a large extent rests on his or her organizational affiliations and resources, such as a wealthy family, an important company or a famous university, even though he or she does not at that occasion act on behalf of the organization. Even children playing in the playground know such things. They may, for instance, tell a playmate not to hit his antagonist because they know that he has two big brothers. Even among children the organizational affiliation and resources make a difference.

Practically everybody has at least two forms of affiliation – citizenship and kinship. Most people have more. Besides their parents and siblings, they may also have a family of their own, with a spouse and children. They may have a job and are perhaps members of one or several voluntary associations such as a party, a trade union, a church or a sports club.

All affiliations set constraints on the interaction with other people. The first things people want to know from you are often your organizational affiliations: where do you work, to whom are you married, what is your citizenship? And even if the others do not know them, your organizational affiliations still put constraints on your options – you have times to keep and you have to account for how you have used organizational resources.

Are there any actions that are not partly on behalf of organizations? Actions where people do not ask where you come from or where you belong? Actions when nobody will ask where you have been, what you have done, what did you do with the money, why did you not come back in time, what did you achieve? Actions you do on your own responsibility with resources you dispose of quite on your own?

Hobos and outlaws are figures often regarded as symbols of freedom and independence, but they are not common. Other examples may be poets and artists. Still, they all have their affiliations, such as family and citizenship, which they cannot totally escape unless they find themselves a sanctuary somewhere. To get away from their affiliations people sometimes try to change their identity and their physical appearance, or even have themselves declared dead.

Now, this is not a matter of either/or. Organizational affiliation constrains interaction with other people in shifting degrees in different situations. It varies with the life cycle. Children and middle aged people tend to be more constrained by organizational affiliations than adolescents and pensioners. It is particularly among the latter two categories that we notice a trend in some affluent countries of an increased share of single households in the population, which denotes a relative independence of affiliations in their social lives.

A more typical image of human behaviour would be in

terms of action on behalf of organizations than an image of autonomous individual actions. In interaction with other people it is more common that people excuse or blame their decisions and actions on their organizational affiliation than make their decisions on their own. 'I can't come, I have to go home.' 'No, I don't have time, I have to go to work.' 'I would like to go there, but my kids don't like it.'

Acting on behalf of organizations is not necessarily bad or negative. It is not that such action is enforced action whereas other forms of action are free. People choose to act on behalf of organizations, since it can be incredibly funny and exciting. It enables people to do things they would not otherwise dream of doing on their own such as being an astronaut and flying to the moon or playing in the final of the world championships in soccer. This is in the idea of collective resources.

What you gain in access to resources and possibilities by organizational affiliations you lose in autonomy and independence. In organizations you can do things you would not be able to do on your own, but you cannot quite choose when you would like to do it, or how often or how much. The organizational context implies a particular rhythm of doing things. Often it means to do things faster, more regularly and more often. What you win in terms of access to resources you lose in spontaneity and autonomy. Organizations may become traps.

Generally it is too strong to say that people act against their will when they act on behalf of organizations. On the other hand, it is rarely accurate to say that they act according to their will. Actions on behalf of organizations are normally, although not necessarily, characterized by a dual involvement; a duality of action. A dual involvement may be expected to be more obvious in relations of employment, when people get paid to do things. But even members of voluntary associations now and then do things on behalf of their organizations that they would rather not do.

In social sciences there is a tendency to see human actors as either determined by a social structure or culture or as rational and free individuals (see Granovetter, 1985). The fact is that though in principle people are free to choose and act, they seldom do, and there are few opportunities to choose organizational affiliation. People are selected into organizations. The social world is certainly made by people, although not according to their own will, but rather through doing what other people tell them to do and often while thinking of something else.

This is not the whole picture. There are moments when people experience a self-realization through acting on behalf of an organization together with friends or colleagues, and there are moments when people are really forced through threats of violence to act against their own will. And sometimes people refuse to obey orders and stop or leave.

## Part organization . . .

When people act on behalf of organizations their abilities and scopes are enhanced; they get extraindividual strength as well as goals and motives. Their behaviour, however, also becomes less human.

Yet, it is not possible to eliminate the human part altogether. The strategy of organizational coordination is usually to minimize the human part to be able to increase control and predictability of actions. Which human qualities are relevant for the action on behalf of the organization varies with the kind of activities involved. People search for the right person for the right job, that is, a person whose human qualities and character fit in with the organizational position. This is not always an easy task. Sometimes physical qualities are decisive, such as strength, sex, or appearance. The leader of a party should have the proper political opinions, of course, as well as be a good leader and manager and be trusted by the members of the party; moreover, he or she should look good on TV. Even in the best of cases there will always be tensions between the organizational requirements and the person involved.

There are basically two approaches in order to minimize the influence of the human part of the organizational centaur; either to subsume and transform as much as possible of the human conduct under the auspices of the organization, thus making it 'part organization', or to separate the human interest as far as possible from organizational activities. The first approach implies as much involvement as possible, the second as little involvement as possible. The problem is that the result is often somewhere in between, with too little involvement as regards the first approach and too much involvement in relation to the second approach.

The first approach implies a high degree of socialization and indoctrination into 'greedy' organizations, 'that are not content with claiming a segment of the energy of individuals but demand their total allegiance' (Coser, 1967: 198). The affiliates should spend as much time as possible in their everyday life within the realms of the organization. This is typical of families and voluntary organizations such as religious bodies, for example, monasteries or sects. Celibacy is a method of preventing influence from another organizational affiliation (see Collins, 1986: 53). The idea is to try to shape the affiliates as much as possible according to organizational demands and tasks. In extreme cases this may lead to mutilations of the body, as in the case of eunuchs (Coser, 1964).

The second approach implies construction of organizational activities that are as independent as possible of whoever is conducting the task. Examples are Taylorism and bureaucracy. In these cases the idea is to create routines that demand as little involvement as possible of the person fulfilling the task thereby increasing substitutability. Clear rules and tasks are ingredients of this approach (see Littler, 1982: 58). Weber wrote about bureaucracy that it functions better 'the more it is dehumanized' (1968: 975). Typically this is an approach in enterprises with routine production, but it may also be applied in the state.

Whatever the approach, the tension between the organizational and the human is always there in all organizations and it is rarely resolved, although it can be expected that a dual involvement is most obvious in forms of employment.

In chapter 1 we analysed four features constitutive of organized interaction between individuals: affiliation, collective resources, substitutability and control. These features can be applied in order to study the bonds of the organizational centaurs. In order to discover the impact of organizational affiliation it is most revealing to select situations where individuals from different organizations interact with one another. In such situations the importance of the organizational bonds becomes obvious. Here are a great variety of social situations ranging from journalists interviewing politicians to soldiers fighting each other in a war, or businessmen negotiating about contracts, or social scientists meeting in a conference.

## Affiliation

The particular organizational affiliation of a person/actor is important when the actions of other people towards that person would differ depending on which organization he or she belongs to. People know this in their interactions and take it for granted and talk in different ways to people with different organizational affiliations; they avoid certain topics or certain names. When one gets to know the people one meets daily, it is as important to learn about their organizational affiliations as their traits of character; whether they are married, whom this or that person is married or related to, whether the person has children or not, where he or she works, whether he or she is a member of a party or a sports club. Affiliations are no less important than age, looks, temperament etc.

A common method to indicate affiliation is through uniforms or garments or labels, for example, a cap or a shirt in the colours of the organization or with the name or logo of the organization printed on it. The pointing out of organizational affiliation through clothing is typical of organizations involved in or prepared for fighting each other, such as armies or football teams. It is also common for employees of the state such as policemen or postmen. Many enterprises, particularly in the service industry, equip their employees with special costumes to advertise their affiliation.

Often when you meet a new person the location reveals the organizational affiliation of that person, for example, the secretary in an office or the person who introduces a meeting in a local union, a doctor behind his desk. On other occasions those accompanying somebody give information about the organizational affiliation, such as a family walking to church or shopping.

A person's surname is another indication of organizational affiliation, which at least in some connections gives good information about civil status and family background. However, some surnames give more information than others; for example, names of noble families, or important families such as Rothschild or Vanderbilt.

Yet, in many situations in your everyday life you meet people whose organizational affiliation you do not know. When people act outside their organizational connection and if they do not wear a uniform or something similar, their exact organizational affiliation is not readily visible. In this type of situation people who act on behalf of organizations will sometimes be required to show a proof of belonging to a certain organization. Plain clothes policemen have to show their badges if they take official action. People collecting money for an organization often show their ID card to prove that they are representatives of that organization. When entering a foreign country some people will be asked to show their passports, and they will be treated differently depending on which country they come from.

Organizational affiliation is not only a certificate attesting education or a professional status or legitimation. An affiliation implies rights and duties towards an organization as well as a certain treatment from people from other organizations. A journalist is not just a journalist. A journalist coming from the biggest newspaper in the country will get different attention from a journalist from a small local newspaper by almost anybody. To some extent this is due to differences in their access to resources.

## Collective resources and power

Equipment such as cars or weapons is one of the most apparent examples of how people's abilities to act are enhanced by organizational resources in ways that create variations between people from different organizations. Motor sport, for example, is an exceptional case among sports since it is so obvious that the contestants have been equipped with resources of different qualities by the teams they belong to. This may be regarded as unfair, but on the other hand it is an extremely common phenomenon although rarely as obvious as in the case of Formula 1.

The effect of unequal resources is not always as obvious as in the cases of cars and weapons, however. Affiliates from organizations with more resources, that is, richer organizations, often get advantages in subtler ways. They can afford to buy better clothes, they can spend more money on representation, they can distribute glossier prints, they can travel more. For university students the extent of financial support they get from their parents is of crucial importance for their chances of entering certain universities.

There is another form of enhancement of the capacity to act on behalf of organizations, which is more difficult to distinguish from personal traits or the human part of the organizational centaur. Resources that a person acquires through socialization in the organization become internalized. The upbringing in the family, the education at school, in-house training, the training one gets in a sports club or in a party, are organizational resources (investments in human capital) that give varying preconditions for actions on behalf of the organization. Actors with better training, better education and more knowledge have many advantages in the interaction with actors from other organizations with fewer resources of this kind. One problem, however, is that these resources or investments are inseparable from the person, which becomes particularly obvious in knowledge-based enterprises. One solution is to ask for transfer sums when an affiliate leaves one organization to join another, as in ice-hockey or soccer. Dowry can also be understood in this way.

Perhaps the most important influence of resources on actions on behalf of organizations is indirect and comes from the potential use of resources. This is the power aspect of resources. When two or several representatives from different organizations meet, in negotiations for example, their interaction can be characterized by inequality even though they have the same equipment and degrees of education. The actor belonging to a bigger organization usually has access to larger resources, which makes his or her arguments more powerful in discussions with people belonging to poorer organizations. A person from a resourceful organization can be nice and charming. He or she does not have to make threats; still, everybody knows that the preconditions for their interaction are constrained by the potential power of their respective organizations. Ultimately, nobody knows exactly what gives power in certain situations, and notions about the potential power of organizations are contested and challenged (this will be discussed thoroughly in chapter 6). The point here is just to underline the fact that interaction between people from different organizations to a large extent is guided by the notions of the potential resources each actor has access to through his or her organizational affiliation. This is true for businessmen from different companies as well as for politicians from different parties and for presidents from different states. The particular bonds of the organizational centaurs are essential for understanding the interaction between them even though they appear to be equals. In a picture the president of the United States does not look much different from the president of Guatemala, but their interaction is certainly dependent upon their respective organizational affiliations and thus different access to resources.

## Substitutability

Organizations become more dependent on affiliates with unique qualities and skills. A person that is difficult to substitute is more difficult to control. A star in a soccer team or a popular politician may take great liberties inside the organization. When procedures to substitute a person are complicated or time-consuming, an election for instance, the power of that person also increases. Royalties are difficult to substitute, because they have to fulfil specific kinship requirements. Generally it holds that the harder it is to find substitutes the more autonomy that person has. Thus, part organization and part human are intertwined. Also a group of persons or a team may make themselves hard to substitute and control, if they monopolize important knowledge, for instance.

Statements or opinions expressed by organizations may not be totally in accordance with those of any one of the affiliates. Decisions are often compromises reached through negotiations and formation of coalitions. Both the programme of a political party and where a family goes for the holidays are expressions of negotiated preferences. It is not the programme nor the holiday any one of the affiliates would have chosen or decided themselves. To what extent can one expect affiliates to uphold the official version? This varies with type of organization and position of the affiliate. People in top positions are more often expected to give the official version. Of course, clergymen are expected to identify themselves with the dogma of their church, but you cannot expect a salesman to say that everything he sells is as good as the advertisements claim. Some organizational representatives do not even pretend to accept the official view. They say: 'I am only doing my job,' or 'If I were to decide I would not do it like this.'

In many organizations there are authorized people in positions to give statements or information, for instance an ambassador. Others are prohibited from saying anything, or at least expected not to publicly announce disagreements within the organization. The official spokesmen may be exchanged, however. A state can get a new government, an enterprise may get a new manager, a party may get a new leadership etc. The promises or the information you had from somebody may suddenly become worthless. It does not matter how trustworthy that person may have been. It is not the same thing to trust a person and to trust an organization. This is one reason why networks resting on personal contacts are vulnerable (see chapter 4).

When you talk to somebody representing an organization you have to find out what part is organization and what part is human, as well as the relative weights of each part. When two politicians from different parties meet, they must try to distinguish between the other's personal view and the official policy of the party.

Interaction among organizational centaurs is complicated since their organizational positions are not always obvious. In some organizations, though, even the position in the hierarchy of that organization is discernible from the uniform or clothing, for example in the army. If you have complaints about service in a restaurant you want to talk to the supervisor or the head waiter, who is probably dressed differently from ordinary waiters.

## Control

Actions of organizational centaurs rest on control. To the degree that they depend upon the organization to be able to come back, their actions on behalf of the organization are checked. When they return they have to account for how they have used resources, what they have achieved and what they have said. In principle, these requirements are the same for politicians, businessmen, diplomats and family members.

Now, as Richard Scott has pointed out, 'so many of the topics discussed in connection with organizations relate more or less directly to the subject of control' (1992: 301). Most of these arguments pertain to relations inside organizations. The autonomy of positions varies depending on the nature of tasks and the place in the internal division of labour (see further chapter 5). Ultimately, the cohesion of an organization rests on the fact that affiliates control each other (see Hechter, 1987).

Control is more problematic when affiliates interact with people who do not belong to the same organization. One interesting discussion on control concerns the so-called 'street-level bureaucrats', that is, public employees who have direct contacts with clients. Even though they work within the premises of the organization their relations with clients are hard to monitor. It can also be difficult to evaluate their performance (Lipsky, 1980; R. Johansson, 1992).

This dilemma is even more pronounced in situations where affiliates of an organization act on their own outside the organization but not outside the organizational context, for example as missionaries, agitators, spies, diplomats, negotiators or salesmen; when affiliates of the same organiz- ation are no longer in face-to-face contact with one another (see Goffmann, 1959: 166). This also goes for family members going shopping or talking to teachers in school. Although people operating on these conditions seem to be acting on their own, they usually have to obey routines for reporting their activities and taking orders. Missionaries are often prohibited to 'marry or in any other way live together with a partner from the host country' (G. Johansson, 1992: 207).

The learning of an organizational culture or ideology becomes most important for affiliates acting to a great extent on their own (see Mintzberg, 1979: 98). Yet, they cannot be left without control altogether. They seldom have full authority to negotiate or use resources. Their decisions have to be confirmed by other affiliates. The division of labour in organizations is in itself a form of control. To increase the dependence of affiliates is another way of controlling them. If the dependence on the organization decreases, however, the bonds between a person and the organization are weakened and thus the conditions for control change. If a spy is offered a residence and a good income in another country the situation may become critical.

Through organizational affiliation human capacities to act are transformed. Some capacities are hindered to some extent such as the capacity to make decisions about your own actions, or to plan your own actions or to say what you think. Other capacities are increased, such as physical ability and strength through military or athletic training. Knowledge is enhanced through education and cultural influences. Organizational affiliation implies a transformation of human capacities by increasing possibilities to operate and calculate while restraining emotional capacities. Actors become stronger, more knowledgeable but less sensitive and less emotionally open, the more they depend on their organizational affiliation.

## Part human . . .

To understand how organizations work it is necessary to know their limits. All organizations are vulnerable and many organizations fail and are dissolved. One of the restrictions in organizations is their difficulties in directing and controlling individual affiliates with feelings, interests and qualities that supersede the realms of the organization. In the long run it happens that people increasingly become accustomed to and moulded into their organizational identities, which may even create an overconformity in adherence to rules and organizational demands (see Merton, 1968). Goffman assumes that people filling positions in the middle ranges of organizations 'most closely approach what the organizations expect them to be' (1968: 182). Consequently, secondary adjustments are least found in the middle of hierarchies and more frequently at the top or at the bottom. However, 'part human' is rarely totally obliterated. From the perspective of the organization the human part of the organizational centaur is often a nuisance.

When acting on behalf of organizations one normally uses only a part of one's human capacities, only part of one's knowledge. Many white-collar professions call for knowledge and mental qualities, whereas in many manual jobs physical powers are used, but opportunities to exercise one's creativity are few. Neither in families do affiliates get to use all their abilities, which is one of the reasons behind the increasing participation of women in wage labour (see Cockburn, 1991: 151). Certain actions on behalf of organizations require a large part of one's personality. A politician, for instance, uses his or her personal charm in order to persuade other people. Personal affection or dislike between party leaders may be important in establishing or preventing cooperation between two parties.

In actions on behalf of organizations the organization determines with whom to interact, with whom to be friendly, whom to help, but it is far from certain that these are the people with whom you would choose to interact if you had your own choice.

Human capacities and needs that are not satisfied or used may give rise to unintended forms of interaction, parallel to, or instead of, action on behalf of the organization. Such interaction may be little things like people sitting around talking to each other instead of working, or people going to political meetings not to discuss politics but to meet friends and gossip. This kind of interaction may certainly be productive and even be encouraged. Generally, though, from the point of view of the organization, it is a disturbance.

Informal relations may also arise in relations between staff and inmates or clients. It is well known from many studies how prison officers develop patterns of interaction with prisoners that deviate from official rules; patterns that give them mutual advantages. Goffman (1968: 89, 184) reports from his study of 'Central Hospital' how the staff used patients as baby-sitters, gardeners or for house painting.

Some affiliates have to interact with representatives from other organizations as customers, business partners or negotiators. Such interaction may lead to close contacts but it must not become too close. As an employee you are expected to be friendly to customers, but you should not become their friend. Organizations have to take measures in order to prevent affiliates in such positions from taking advantage of their contacts. An example of such a gain is a bribe.

Several writers have pointed out the importance of personal relations, that is, networks, in contacts between organizations. Salespeople often know each other well. 'In a general way, there is evidence all around us of the extent to which business relations are mixed up with social ones' (Granovetter, 1985: 495). Granovetter argues against a simplified way of looking at distinctions between markets and hierarchies. According to him, they are both embedded in social relations. But this argument cannot be taken too far. If organizations are too embedded in networks they will be dissolved. There is a limit to the embeddedness of organizations.

Even in situations when representatives from different organizations are expected to fight each other they may refuse and start to cooperate. This rarely happens in soccer, although there have been cases of fixed matches. Axelrod (1984: 73–87) gives the example of the trench warfare during the First World War, where German and French soldiers cooperated in not opening fire against each other. It happens that troops refuse to shoot at demonstrators or protesters, since they identify themselves with the protesters. One example of this was the failed *coup d'état* in Moscow in August 1991. In order to avoid refusals from subordinates commanders may recruit troops from other parts of the country, who may even be unable to speak with the protesters. That is one strategy to minimize the influence of the human part of soldiers.

In families sex and sexuality are explicit parts of the organizational schemes. In this respect sex is 'part organization'. Sexuality is in a sense turned into action on behalf of the organization, actions that spouses expect of each other. In several other types of organization sex and sexuality are used to design tasks and positions or to attract customers or spectators. 'The "sexy" uniform of a club waitress, for instance, exploits for profit both her female sexuality and the male sexuality of the client' (Cockburn, 1991: 149).

When sex is not explicitly part organization it is part human, and as such it plays a role in many organizations in the interaction between affiliates and in relations with customers or clients. Cynthia Cockburn writes: 'All organizations must generate policies for handling sexual affairs and marriages among their employees if they are to avoid disruption, loss of output and failure of managerial control' (1991: 151). In her book *In the Way of Women*, Cockburn discusses sexual harassment in work organizations as a way for male employees to assert their position of power (1991: 64, 142). The mix of men and women in similar positions affects actions on behalf of organizations. When the proportion of women is small their visibility as women increases. They become tokens as part human and not as part organization (see Kanter, 1977: 207–12).

Likewise in relations between affiliates and clients there may occur situations where sexuality impinges upon the organizational interaction. Patients may ask nurses for sexual services. In psychotherapy it happens that the close relationship between the therapist and the client is changed into a relationship of love and sexuality, which often leaves the client in a worse state than before the therapy started. In interaction between neighbouring families there are often informal rules prohibiting too close relations between the husband of one family and the wife of another. It is very rare for a man to be able to call on a woman in a neighbouring family if she is alone at home (see Rosengren, 1991).

The human part of the organizational centaur sets limits to demands on actions on behalf of an organization. Affiliates cannot be made to do anything or act against personal convictions. Political parties often compromise about their demands, and politicians now and then have to argue in favour of decisions they do not embrace themselves. Sometimes a member of a party or a government may think that compromises have gone too far, and as a result he or she leaves the party. Sometimes employees quit their jobs when conditions become unbearable even though they do not have a new job to go to. Reactions of this kind may also be collective, such as in wildcat strikes.

There is always a tension between organizational demands and the human mind and body. When and how people react to such tensions is contingent on the exact situation and constellation of other organizations. The threshold to leave an organization is lower the more alternatives there are, and the lower the dependence on organizational resources is. Dependence on organizational resources within families can be seen as proportionate to the incomes of the spouses (Hobson, 1990), and this often affects divorces. Reactions of dissatisfaction may be discussed in terms of exit and voice (see Hirschman, 1970, 1981; see also Ahrne, 1990: 84–90).

# 3

# THE ORGANIZED TRANSFORMATION OF ACTION INTO PROCESS

## Filtered actions

Through actions on behalf of organizations human action is transformed into social processes. In organizations actions are coordinated and thus accumulated in order to exceed what individuals acting on their own can possibly accomplish even if they try just as much. Processes such as modernization, the division of labour, bureaucratization, colonization, democratization or globalization unfold through the growth, spread and dissolution of organizations. Social change happens through interaction between organizations and the movements of people between organizations through entries and exits (see chapters 6 and 7).

Place and time are basic elements in organizational coordination. Organization is an answer to what puzzles Giddens (1990a: 14) 'how social systems "bind" time and space'. Perhaps the simplest form of coordination is to gather a number of people in a particular place to combine their strength, for example in rowing a boat. Their strength is multiplied. Another method of coordination is succession, for instance in keeping a fire burning. It means that the action of the previous person is continued longer than would have been possible on his or her own. The most typical form of coordination, however, rests on specialization or a division of labour where different actions of different people are complementary. Yet, the crucial moment is the coordination in place and time. The results of each action within a division of labour are useless without coordination, that is, without being combined with the work of the others. In most organizations all three methods of coordination – multiplication, succession and specialization – are practised in various combinations.

For an outsider the effects of the coordination of actions on behalf of organizations appear more coherent than they are. The outsider may thus perceive the organization as a single actor, but the closer you come the more fragmented it becomes. It is like watching performances where the coordinated waving of flags or papers by thousands of people in a sports arena at a distance appear as pictures or letters forming words that change. The closer you get the more difficult it becomes to discern the patterns and you only see a lot of people waving flags. It is the same with social processes.

Actions are rarely one-dimensional or unambiguous. People tend to do two or more things at the same time and often they think of something else. You wash the dishes and talk to your children or you eat lunch and negotiate with a business partner. The association between personal motives and actions on behalf of an organization is seldom straightforward. Motives and interests are often indirectly related to organizational actions.

While the accumulated results of actions on behalf of organizations form social processes other dimensions of actions and thoughts fade away. Doubt, hesitance, anger, repentance, tears, or laughter are not accumulated. Secondary adjustments and expressions given off are not accumulated. This is not to say that motives and feelings are insignificant. They may affect how people act on behalf of organizations.

When actions are transformed into processes part of what

you do is lost. In organizations actions are filtered, some aspects of human actions are accumulated and transformed into social processes whereas other dimensions may only last in the memory of a colleague or a customer. The equipment and tasks of organizational positions are the filters that separate actions on behalf of organizations from other aspects of actions.

In terms of human action this means that actions on behalf of organizations generate social change. People change the world while fulfilling their routines. Social change does not necessarily imply changed routines. A 'bureaucrat' is often an agent of change. In families as well as in business enterprises reproduction of the organization causes social change.

The growth of enterprises as well as voluntary associations presupposes recruitment of new affiliates. Thus, to join organizations, to take a job or to become a member of a voluntary organization, or to leave them are important processes of change. Yet, inside organizations people change the social landscape by following rules and fulfilling their tasks.

There is a moment of dual involvement in all social processes. Social processes are continuously enacted. All decisions and all manifestations of power in organizations ultimately rely on individual actions filtered through organizational positions. This goes for presidents as well as workers, for generals as well as for soldiers. Macro-events are staged from an everyday life perspective circumscribed by organizational positions.

Organizational power rests upon the assumption that affiliates do come back. To be regarded as powerful an organization needs to demonstrate its ability to make its affiliates do certain things, to mobilize soldiers, to mobilize members in a strike, or to make workers work harder. The point is that power rests on actual or possible coordinated actions.

When it comes to collective decisions affiliates have to be mobilized and show up. Although the strength of each party in the parliament is known in terms of number of seats, members must show up to vote. If some members fail to show up the outcome may be unexpected. Power on paper is not enough.

The popular 'garbage can theory' of decisions builds upon the everyday life realities of decision-making. Collective decisions are made in a certain place at a certain time and 'who is attending to what and when' are critical moments in explanations of decisions in organizations (March and Olsen, 1982: 38). Which people are present to make a specific decision can to some extent depend upon other demands and tasks (Cohen et al., 1982: 27). Since decision-making is enacted, it is contingent upon specific individuals and their schedules.

## Types of activity and types of organization

Actions, that is, things that people do, can be described in terms of physical movements or in terms of motives and functions related to needs. There are simple descriptions of actions such as walking, talking, eating, lifting etc. There are also more complicated descriptions of actions such as playing, thinking, working, teaching. There are terms to describe spheres or types of activities such as education, religion, politics, production, leisure. We do not intend to analyse different types of activities here. We only want to argue that there is no necessary connection between type of activity and type of organization. Both in the context of simple actions such as talking or running, as well as more complex spheres of action such as education, production, or religion, it is a matter of experience that they are performed in all types of organization. Productive activities as well as religious activities are constantly performed in families, in states, in voluntary associations, and in business enterprises. The same organization can embrace a number of activities at the same time, and almost all activities can take place in all types of organization.

In specifying what constitutes a society or a system sociologists have mixed organizations and activities in elusive definitions or taxonomies. Gerth and Mills (1970: 26) refer to five institutional orders: political, economic, military, kinship and religious orders. As institutional orders Giddens (1984: 31) names: symbolic orders, political, economic and legal institutions. In his book *Consequences of Modernity*, Giddens (1990a: 59) talks about 'the institutional dimensions of modernity': surveillance, capitalism, industrialism and military power. Michael Mann (1986: 28) distinguishes four networks of power: ideological, economic, military and political power.

The best-known classification of functions or activities as spheres of society is that of Talcott Parsons. In his later works he treats 'a society as analytically divisible into four *primary* subsystems' (1971: 10). These are: societal community, pattern maintenance or fiduciary, polity, economy. The four subsystems correspond to four primary functions: integration, pattern maintenance, goal attainment and adaptation. Parsons states that the divisions among subsystems of action and subsystems of society are rarely very neat. He admits that there is a considerable overlap between them. Yet, he constructs an image of society that rests on basic primary functions. It seems that, despite their strong rejection of Parsons's functionalism, theorists such as Mills and Giddens have not been able to distance themselves from this mode of representing society.

Organizations determine conditions for actions through resources, rules and power. The same type of activity can happen in several organizational contexts and the same organization may embrace many types of activity. Spheres of activity such as education, production, religion, care, sport etc. can be organized into any type of organization. Yet, we cannot say that an activity is totally unaffected by the organizational form.

Organization is a basic social figuration with variations according to form of affiliation and nature of the collective resources. We have distinguished between several forms of affiliation: kinship and marriage, citizenship, membership and ownership. These forms of affiliation imply formal rights; formal affiliates are mandators of their organization (see Abrahamsson, 1993: 14). Affiliation to an organization is a formal category, but this does not imply that everything that goes on inside organizations follows formal rules. A formal affiliation does not preclude informal actions within organizations.

Kinship and citizenship are compulsory forms of affiliation, whereas marriage, membership and ownership are voluntary. Today the four main types of organization are: families, states, voluntary associations and business enterprises. Employment is a secondary form of affiliation that pertains to all four of these organizations, although it is typically associated with business enterprises.

The form of affiliation and resources gives different flexibility to different types of organization. States are the least flexible of organizations, since they can neither choose nor dispose of citizens in an easy way. Because of the nature of their collective resources states are territorially defined and bound. Business enterprises, on the other hand, can dispose of employees and change owners at short notice. They also have good possibilities, within certain limits, to choose their location and what activities to engage in (see Ahrne, 1990: 60–5).

Forms of affiliation also make a difference in the activity. Eating dinner at home with your family is not quite like eating dinner with a business partner. Education within the realms of the family is not quite the same thing as education in business enterprises or within state organizations owing to the affiliational bonds of people involved in the interaction. The difference between amateurs and professionals in sport is a difference in terms of membership versus employment. The professionalization of sport has been contested. In the late nineteenth century many soccer clubs were opposed to the introduction of professional players arguing that it would change the character of the game (Vamplew, 1988: 191–4).

Both ownership and employment have a negative connotation in that they imply doing things for the sake of earning money without a real interest in the activity itself. On the other hand, ownership is expected to encourage efficiency through the profit motive. Employment often implies a notion of professionalism, that is, a high competence. Voluntary membership implies strong commitment and often benevolence. Kinship is supposed to imply strong affections.

Often families are regarded as qualitatively different from other organizations. Coleman, for instance, writes about the conflict between a primordial structure including the family and a 'purposive structure' of economic organizations and governments (1990: 584). Elsewhere in the sociological literature families are often classified as 'primary groups'.

In his book *Social Organization*, Cooley (1914: 23) defines primary groups as 'those characterized by intimate face-to-face association and cooperation'. Among the most important primary groups, he mentions the family, the playgroup of children and the neighbourhood. But he recognizes several other forms of primary associations, such as clubs, fraternal societies, colleges, that are 'based on congeniality, which may give rise to real intimacy' (1914: 26). Thus, Cooley's definition of primary groups does not distinguish families from other organizations. His definition of a primary group is based on a type of relation, intimacy, which can exist among people in all types of organization.

Historically, family and kinship structures have been involved in all kinds of activity: economic, political, religious, cultural, educational etc. At times, families have been reduced considerably in terms of activities, for instance in the kibbutz, where children were only supposed to spend a couple of hours each day with their parents, and all children lived in separate houses. These rules have gradually become loosened and an increasing 'familism' has occurred (Tiger and Sheper, 1975: 225).

It is through organizational forms that human actions are transformed into social processes. In the remainder of the chapter we will briefly describe the four main types of organization existing today in order to analyse how the basic features of organization – affiliation, collective resources, substitutability and control – have changed form, and how types of activity have shifted across types of organization. In the course of this process human everyday actions have been divisionalized into separate organizational spheres. As global society is becoming an integrated web of overlapping organizations, everyday lives of ordinary people are disintegrated into a number of organizational affiliations with different tasks and expectations and different forms of control and gate-keeping. What is integration in terms of organizations is disintegration in terms of the coherence of human action. Different organizations have come closer to each other in competition or cooperation, while everyday lives are lived in a wider and more diverse context of organizational affiliations.

## Kinship, family and marriage

The emergence of primal families dates back to long before human history or the full development of language and symbolization (Keesing, 1975: 4). Families and kinship are inseparable from the biological evolution of mankind. Among the biological elements that may explain the origin of families are the development of continual sexual receptivity of the female and a prolonging of infantile dependence. With the origin of the family a principle of sharing of resources evolved, a first division of labour (Keesing, 1975: 3).

Families as organizations are originally connected with sexuality. Sexual relations do not happen only inside families, but there is no other type of organization that has organized sexual relations. This is one of the few exceptions to the fact that all types of activity can be organized into all types of organization.

In the course of time there have existed a large variation in rules of marriage and descent. Such rules, however, are 'continually open to negotiation – with rules being created, broken, redefined, and elaborated' (Keesing, 1975: 142). Yet, the elementary forms of family and kinship have remained the same.

In the sociological literature there is a debate on how to define and conceptualize family and kinship. Recently, however, Collins and Coltrane have presented a 'property theory of the family' that well captures the essentials of families as organizations. The first element of the theory is the sexual relation. 'If we look at who has the exclusive right to sexual intercourse with whom, we will find the core of the family' (Collins and Coltrane, 1991: 74, 78). Rules around this relationship vary, but in all families sexual relations are regulated in terms of affiliation and exclusion, and there is always a degree of control involved in these matters. This is what fidelity is all about. Even families consisting of one parent and children are organized around sexuality in a negative sense through the prohibition against incest.

The second element of the theory is economic property. A family is an economic unit in the sense that economic resources are shared among family members. They have rights and duties to contribute to the collective resources of the family and to get their livelihood. Here Collins and Coltrane mention 'the family's income and the household labor involved in running an unpaid domestic business of cooking, cleaning, lodging and child care' (1991: 78). In all families there is a division of labour and of resources.

A common part of most definitions of the family is its domestic unity (see for instance Popenoe, 1988: 6). It is true that most families share resources in the form of a common home. This is not necessary, though. Families may keep together without living together for long periods. Families are not territorially bound; as an organizational form it is mobile. Other elements of Popenoe's (1988: 6) definition of families such as affection and provision of care are not necessary either, and are not unique to families.

The third element of the theory bridges the gap between family and kinship through 'the intergenerational linkage of property rights and obligations between parents and children' (Collins and Coltrane, 1991: 75). The survival of a family as an organization happens through inheritance of collective resources, and the substitutability of family members follows rights of inheritance.

Definitions of kinship and family have to be interconnected; without families there is no kinship but without kinship there is no family. Kinship is compulsory and ascribed. The criterion of inclusion is consanguinity. Adoption of children is unusual and can be regarded as an inverted form of gaining kinship (see Verdon, 1981: 815). Marriage, on the other hand, is voluntary, at least in principle. Even though it may not be a voluntary decision on the part of the bride or bridegroom, it is a voluntary decision from her or his parents to arrange the marriage (see Kapur, 1973: 250–2). Nowadays, often, kinship is above all a matter of relations between parents and married children as well as relations between siblings (Morgan, 1975: 81). In most countries of the world, however, kinship is more than that and holds a greater importance than in Western Europe and North America. The kinship relations that are relevant vary across time and space.

It is important to emphasize the interconnectedness of kinship and family. Kinship is a phenomenon that does not fit in well with notions of modernity, and it has been regarded as a survival from premodern times. Sometimes the conjugal family has been supposed to be the only remaining form of family, and the remaining importance of kinship relations has been a surprise for many. Yet, kinship relations have been demonstrated to be of great significance in many spheres of life (see Morgan, 1975; Höllinger and Haller, 1990). Kinship is a form of organization with an ascribed form of affiliation in terms of consanguinity. The basic structure of kinship is formal (Harris, 1990: 58, 96). Yet, in many situations the relevance of specific kinship relations is not obvious. 'The closer the kin, the stronger the obligations' (Harris, 1990: 62). Relations to grandparents or siblings are generally quite strong and demanding whereas relations to cousins or second cousins are often rather loose and often chosen on the basis of personal liking even though the underlying relationship is ascribed (Harris, 1990: 63). Yet, it is the latent kinship connection that makes the choice of a relationship feasible at all.

In the long run it is obvious that family and kinship have lost in importance to other types of organization. People's dependence on their family is not as total as it has been. Nevertheless, it is probably true that the decline of the family as a type of organization has often been overestimated. Families and kinship still play an important role both in people's everyday lives and as part of social processes.

Even though the forms of families to a large extent are institutionalized in terms of legislation and customs, these forms are not planned and laid out by states through political decisions. The rules and habits of family formation change despite institutionalized rules and legislation. One example is the gradual development of forms of cohabitation among young couples in Sweden and several other Western European countries. Cohabitation without a formal marriage ceremony implies an exclusion in terms of sexual relations and it also involves sharing of resources (see Collins and Coltrane, 1991: 72). Thus, it is a family. Only later did the legislation of the state adapt itself to the new form of family that slowly emerged. Families are not only results of influence from other organizations. 'The family itself is capable of actions and modifications which in turn produce a transformation in its environment' (Sgritta, 1989: 73).

## Citizenship and states

A direct relationship between a state organization and its citizens is a relatively recent phenomenon. Citizenship was 'an invention of the French Revolution' (Brubaker, 1992: 35). State organizations were not originally constituted on individual affiliation.

Before the invention or introduction of direct citizenship states functioned through forms of indirect rule. They ruled through 'powerful intermediaries' (Tilly, 1990: 104). Those intermediaries were of different character: landlords, urban oligarchies or independent professional warriors. Individual affiliation was accomplished at a 'substate level' (Brubaker, 1992: 36).

In his book *Coercion, Capital and European States AD 990–1990*, Tilly gives an organizational definition of states 'as coercion-wielding organizations that are distinct from households and kinship groups' (1990: 1). This definition does not include citizenship since it covers both early and modern states. The first states were thus not organizations in the sense that they were constructed on individual affiliation. They were rather organizations of organizations, that is, coalitions or alliances of separate organizations (for a discussion of 'organizations of organizations' see chapter 7). Originally, states only covered small parts of the world, often as city-states. The global coverage of states is a phenomenon of the twentieth century.

The decisive step towards a system of citizenship and direct rule was taken in the course of the French revolution when the revolutionaries faced the problem of governing without intermediaries. The revolutionary administration reorganized the country into regional administrative units and 'gave a common substance to citizenship: civil equality' (Brubaker, 1992: 48 and Tilly, 1990: 109). From France and through French conquests the idea of citizenship and the practice of direct rule was spread and imposed throughout Europe (Tilly 1990: 107). This was a process of rapid isomorphism (see further chapter 7). The introduction of direct rule implied new forms of control and surveillance (see Foucault on 'examination', 1975: 184ff.). New direct relations between states and their affiliates created pronounced differences between citizens and non-citizens of each state. Foreigners were increasingly treated as 'distinctive kinds of people' (Tilly, 1990: 116).

From its very beginning the new citizenship in France was

not exclusive. 'In its early stages the Revolution was ostentatiously cosmopolitan' (Brubaker, 1992: 44). Foreigners were welcome and held the same rights as the newly liberated Frenchmen. The emerging nationalism was caused by threats against the revolution that were directed from abroad, but also from within the country.

Like all forms of affiliation citizenship is 'an institution at once inclusive and exclusive' (Brubaker, 1992: 52). The emergence of exclusive citizenship can be studied in several German states in the first half of the nineteenth century. The introduction of citizenship was a means of protection against poor people from other German states. Movements between states were regulated through common agreements on expulsion practices of each state. This implied defining citizenship not in terms of residence but in terms of formal affiliation (Brubaker, 1992: 63, 69–71).

As organizations, states are defined both according to territory and citizenry (see Weber, 1968: 56). Only residence within the territory, however, does not imply full citizenship rights, although permanent residence may sometimes imply certain social rights. The general principle for acquiring citizenship in a particular state is through ascription, that is to say, one is born into citizenship. Yet, in all states there is some possibility of becoming a citizen through naturalization. The principles and practices of naturalization vary greatly between countries (see Brubaker, 1992: 33).

States are bound to a territory and cannot easily move. Neither are the citizens of a state selected or chosen and citizens are hard to expel, at least in larger numbers. Thus, state organizations are the least flexible of organizations. A state is an organization that cannot choose where to operate nor choose the number of its affiliates nor who those affiliates are. These preconditions can to a large extent explain the inertia of the state.

Yet, in terms of activities states can do almost anything. One can hardly think of any type of human activity that has not at some time or the other been organized by the state.

States are continuously involved in organizing education, religion, culture, production, entertainment etc. The state can do anything, but not always in the best or most efficient way. It has 'strong thumbs, but no fingers' (Lindblom, 1977: 65).

Often the state is defined in terms of the legitimate use of physical force (see Weber, 1968: 54). A state is not the only organization that uses physical force, however. There are several voluntary political organizations in the world at present that use physical force in their activities. The matter of legitimacy can always be contested and the question asked, legitimate for whom? Generally, however, states do have the strongest means to use physical force. It is an important part of a state's power, and the origins and development of the state as an organization can partly be understood in relation to warfare and the investment in weapons as collective resources (Tilly, 1990). The primary means for states to collect resources is through taxation of citizens.

What a state does, what activities it organizes, is a matter of struggle among citizens and organizations within or outside its territory. Activities are results of 'multiple bargains' (Tilly, 1990: 102). In his well-known article 'Citizenship and social class', T.H. Marshall regards social rights as 'achieved through a compromise which is not dictated by logic' (1965: 134). A state cannot a priori be regarded as performing activities or functions in the interests of certain classes or groups (see Poulantzas, 1978: 12). When states are labelled democratic states, welfare states or capitalist states, such labels cover only parts of the activities performed by a state and often not the most important ones.

## Ownership, firms and employment

Unlike in the case of family and kinship, there is little controversy about what constitutes a firm or an enterprise. Definitions seem to be straightforward and taken for granted.

Ownership is the constitutional form of affiliation in firms or business enterprises. Owners are mandators and have the rights of control, although this has at times been severely contested. As firms have grown, they have acquired many more employees than owners. The implication of this development has been that 'the management of the enterprise became separated from its ownership' (Chandler, 1977: 9). It is hardly correct to talk about private ownership. Ownership is usually collective in the sense that owners own a firm together with other owners.

The emergence of firms can be dated back at least a thousand years to maritime firms in what today is Italy. Such firms were short-term arrangements lasting not more than months. Inland firms based on families proved to be stronger and more persistent (see Braudel, 1982: 433–6). The original forms of firms were rigorous. According to Chandler, business enterprises in North America in the 1790s 'relied entirely on commercial practices and procedures invented and perfected centuries earlier by British, Dutch, and Italian merchants' (1977: 16).

Out of the family firms there slowly developed a form of 'limited partnership firm' that spread across Europe. There were also early joint-stock companies, the spread of which was slower. Braudel (1982: 442) regards these as 'three generations of firms'. He emphasizes the importance of kinship relations as well as networks for the emergence of firms (see Chandler, 1977: 18; Zucker, 1983: 26). The emergence of capitalist production has also been traced back to Christian monasticism, particularly Cistercians (Collins, 1986: 52–4). It was probably not until the second half of the nineteenth century that joint-stock companies came to be the regular form of firms, often though with a substantial part of the shares in the ownership of one family. During the past hundred years joint-stock ownership has grown tremendously.

Firms originated from trade activities. The growth of firms, however, into capitalist enterprises took place through involvement in production. It was first of all in production that employment emerged as a form of affiliation. Employment evolved gradually to become a generalized form of voluntary affiliation with wages paid in cash. Origins of employment relations came from several types of organization: the guild system, the master–servant relation, and the state. Many forms of embryonic employment such as domestic service or apprenticeship implied subordination not only during work but also in private life (Veneziani, 1986: 38–47).

Craig Littler (1982: 65–6) mentions three forms of social relations that were carried over into early production organizations: familial relations and control, the master craftsman role, and team work on a gang basis with a gang boss. Direct employment relations were at first most common in new large-scale industries and in monopolistic service organizations such as post offices and railways. Indirect employment relations with sub-contractors remained for a long time in industries founded on a craft basis such as building and metal industries (Littler, 1982: 71). Often it was easier to establish an employment relationship in the countryside, where inexperienced workers 'offered a tabula rasa' (Landes, 1986: 599) in contrast to skilled workers in cities who had acquired habits and standards that were hard to overcome. By the last quarter of the nineteenth century, however, most forms of subcontracting were on a decline in British factories (Littler, 1982: 79).

Gradually employment came to be the common form of affiliation in firms and business enterprises (see Zucker, 1983: 15). Employment is not limited to business enterprises, however, and it does not constitute a specific type of organization. Employment pertains to all types of organization. There are employees in states as well as in voluntary associations and in families.

From being largely a domestic relationship employment has been turned into a relationship including freedom of movement, and it is a voluntary form of affiliation. Yet, the employment relationship in itself is a relation of subordination presupposing the power and authority exercised by an employer (Veneziani, 1986: 65, 71). Employment relations are not just like commercial contracts. Through employment the employee is at the disposal of the employer during a certain period of time to perform various activities within a zone of indifference. In this sense an employment relationship gives more flexibility for the employer to adapt activities to changing circumstances than a business contract (see Williamson, 1985: 249; Stinchcombe, 1990: 201).

Employment is a form of interaction in organized settings that can include almost any sphere of human activity. Employment is not the same thing as work, which is rather a type of activity. And work itself is notoriously difficult to define (see Pahl, 1984: 186–9). Employment as a form of affiliation is a clear formal relationship independent of type of activity.

As organizations, firms are more flexible than either families or states. Employers can choose their employees and also to a large extent dismiss them. Owners of enterprises can choose the activities they want to be involved in. Ownership is transferable to other people. Moreover, in principle, the capital of a business enterprise is movable. Production sites can be sold or moved. All forms of business property are not movable to the same extent, yet, mines or factories can be abandoned or closed down. A state cannot abandon any of its territory once it has been claimed. Braudel (1982: 433) emphasizes as a most remarkable feature of the development of capitalist production in business enterprises: 'its unlimited flexibility, its capacity for change and adaption'.

## Membership and voluntary associations

Membership is voluntary in the sense that it is not ascribed upon a person by birth like citizenship and kinship. As the mandatory form of affiliation in voluntary associations, membership implies rights to take part in the selection of representatives or leaders and in decisions on strategies and goals. Definitions of voluntary associations typically emphasize that members are not paid, 'financially recompensed' (Knoke, 1986: 2), for their participation.

Employees of a voluntary association do not have the same rights as members, but employees can also be members. This is not to deny that, in practice, often one or a few members have a greater influence than others within a voluntary association (see further chapter 5).

Although membership is voluntary, a particular association will not accept just anybody as a member. In most of them you have to apply for membership and fulfil certain requirements. In some associations you have to be elected as a member or be recommended by a previous member. A party does not accept as members persons who are already members of another party; the same goes for churches. Associations are able to exclude members who do not live up to basic requirements or who hurt the organization through their behaviour or opinions.

In the discussion around voluntary associations there is some confusion about the idea of movements. Many voluntary associations prefer to describe themselves as movements or 'new social movements'. In contrast to organizations movements are seen as fluid and lacking boundaries (see Klandermans and Tarrow, 1988: 15; Dalton et al., 1990: 13). In summarizing a number of case studies and comparative research on movements and associations, many writers have concluded that it is important to distinguish between organizations and movements. Social movement is a wider concept that pertains to both a set of opinions, perhaps a lifestyle, and to networks of supporters. Social movements such as the peace movement or the civil rights movement in the United States have often been made out of coalitions of several existing organizations (see Rochon, 1990 and Klandermans, 1990). Klandermans and Tarrow concluded that it is most appropriate 'to focus on both organizational members and external participants, leaving as an empirical question the importance of the two in each movement' (1988: 16; cf. McCarthy and Zald, 1987a: 29–30).

Among voluntary associations there is a difference between 'expressive' and 'social influence' associations (Rose, 1954: 73). The former are primarily devoted to expressive purposes of the members themselves, whereas the latter type is directed towards the outside. Probably the latter form of association is more common, and these are the voluntary organizations that are often 'carriers of social movements' (Gamson, 1987: 1). Here we find organizations such as unions, peace organizations or environmental organizations. It may happen that the boundary between an association and the outside is rather fluid in newly created associations, and that they can be described as 'networks of networks' (Kuechler and Dalton,1990: 289).

Most of the research on voluntary associations has found that fluid organizations have problems when it comes to strategical decisions. In the long run they 'are faced with an insoluble predicament' (Kuechler and Dalton, 1990: 288). When it comes to decisions on what to do in a practical political question or how to use collective resources, all organizations are bound to set definite limits on who is allowed to take part in the decision-making process and who is not. No organization can afford to let simply anyone be present and have a vote; it makes it extremely vulnerable to enemies. There will be a time in the development of any organization when members realize that they have to have closed meetings where the identities of those present are controlled. But very little research has been conducted on decision-making in voluntary associations (see Knoke, 1986: 11).

Voluntary membership and associations are social inventions following from conditions in England in the revolutionary period in the second half of the seventeenth century. D.B. Robertson writes about the organizational explosion that came to 'cushion the space between the individual or the family and the powerful modern state or monarch' (1966: 110; cf. Roberts, 1972: 17). The new associations provided 'a refuge from the anonymous' in the growing towns and cities (Jacob, 1991: 220). Probably the best known and most widely spread of these new associations is the Freemasons. Freemasonry originated in the guild system, which evolved into several forms of affiliation, both employment and membership. Most of the new associations were political in a general sense and formed important parts of a new secular culture. The new form of affiliation, membership, was an essential element in this process. According to Margaret Jacob in her book *Living the Enlightenment*, the form of Freemason lodges transmitted a political message 'based upon constitutionalism, which gradually turned against traditional privileges and established, hierarchical authority' (1991: 51). The Enlightenment was organized.

Freemasons were among the first voluntary associations to spread to continental Europe and to North America. Despite their ability to spread, the basis of voluntary associations is locally determined. All voluntary associations are regionally organized into localities, districts, regions etc. The importance of membership participation and the principal equality among members make the local connection strong. Voluntary associations are spread through setting up new local organizations and recruiting new members, but they cannot be moved. In comparison with both firms and families, voluntary associations are spatially stable. A trade union cannot follow an enterprise that is changing location (see further chapter 7).

Voluntary associations can be engaged in a great number of activities. Tocqueville noted this in the United States in the early nineteenth century: 'The Americans make associations to give entertainments, to found establishments, for education, to build inns, to construct churches, to diffuse books, to send missionaries to the antipodes: and in this manner they found hospitals, prisons and schools' (1961: 128).

An issue concerning the implication of form of affiliation in voluntary associations is the discussion around employment. Many members fear that employees will get too much influence and change the character of activities from being idealistic and voluntary to being only for the sake of earning money. Michels (1962: 135–40), however, makes some interesting arguments in favour of paying representatives. He argues that this would enable people who otherwise could not afford to participate to fully make use of their membership. McCarthy and Zald (1987b: 374–80) discuss a recent hybrid form of voluntary associations that they call 'professional social movements'. They are run by professional organizers and the only activity of members is to pay membership fees.

# 4

# OUTSIDE ORGANIZATIONS

## Life in semi-organized fields

A semi-organized field is maintained and controlled by an organization or through cooperation of several organizations, as in a shopping mall. Semi-organized fields are set up in order to foster exchange between an organization and the surrounding social landscape. Management and control of people in a semi-organized field is different from that of affiliates. Functionaries are not supposed to select customers, passengers or visitors or tell them what to do, only what they cannot do. If there is a queue to the entrance people are admitted according to their position in the line. In semi-organized fields representatives of the organization are not supposed to pick people from a queue. At times, though, restaurant owners let people who are recognized as 'special guests' pass a queue. Restaurants where the owners want to control their 'guests' are often turned into clubs with membership cards. To become affiliated to an organization, however, there are no queues. For affiliation people are selected at the mercy of those running the organization. There are exceptions: golf clubs, for instance, sometimes have waiting lists, but employers rarely have.

Shop owners can locate the premises in certain areas and adjust to the tastes of certain people. In principle, though, a semi-organized field is open to everybody. People in the semi-organized field are anonymous and they are not asked to identify themselves. Customers, passengers or spectators are usually unknown to each other. Sometimes you may recognize a person going on the bus to the city for many years, but you do not know his or her name.

Yet, in some places people are excluded from entering a semi-organized field because of requirements concerning outer attributes such as clothing or age. Some restaurants require guests to be properly dressed. If you want to enter buildings of religious organizations, you often have to follow certain rules about your dress such as not wearing a hat or a cap or not wearing shoes. To enter museums, cinemas or theatres you will usually have to pay.

People going into a supermarket, a boutique or an art gallery have no commitment to buy anything, and people visiting a political meeting have no commitment to become convinced about the message. Generally, in semi-organized fields people do not promise to come back. A shop owner is not supposed to scold people who do not come regularly. At most he or she can appeal to them to come back or the shop will have to close down. If you are a member of a cooperative, however, there is a commitment to shop there on a regular basis, at least in small cooperatives. If you are a sympathizer of a political party the functionaries of that party are happy when you turn up for a meeting or a demonstration. Once you become a member, however, they do not rejoice when you show up, but they will rebuke you when you fail to come.

There is control in semi-organized fields, too, although the control exercised does not have the same character as inside organizations; it is not recorded. When you leave a supermarket you have to show the goods you want to buy to the cashier. If you go by train your ticket is checked by an official. But your achievements are not recorded, and you are not rewarded for good performance or initiative. Nobody will ask for you if you do not come. You are not expected.

Semi-organized fields rely heavily on self-control, 'to look and not to snatch, to move casually without interrupting the flow, to gaze with controlled enthusiasm and a blasé outlook, to observe others without being seen' (Featherstone, 1991: 24). For those who do not live up to this discipline, as Mike Featherstone observes, 'there lurks in the background surveillance by security guards and remote-control cameras' (1991: 25).

In many organizations techniques are used to try to draw customers, visitors, passengers or readers closer to the organization, to tie them up without making them into affiliates. Reductions in prices are offered to customers who buy for a certain amount of money during a month or a year. A monthly card on the bus is cheaper than the ticket you buy each day. At times, semi-organized fields are quasi-organizations such as The Book of the Month Club, where 'members' commit themselves to buy a book each month, but they have no rights to influence which books are published.

All firms do not rely on semi-organized fields to the same extent as shops, supermarkets or cinemas. Enterprises in production such as steel mills sell their products directly to other enterprises. They have direct relations with their customers. But they also have semi-organized fields, for instance, during trade fairs. A nuclear plant may have a public exhibition on their premises in order to convince people of the safety of their operations.

People moving around in semi-organized fields do not cooperate, and they are often described as a mass. When people in a mass perceive common threats or interests, however, they can be united into a fused group (Sartre, 1976: 361), which may develop into a spontaneous protest movement. In rare instances the interaction of unknown people can lead to spontaneous movements that function for some time, maybe a month, maybe a year, without being organized as long as the spontaneous interest remains strong. Unless it is turned into a proper organization, however, it is bound to perish.

Outside all organizations, when you are not among friends and not acting on behalf of any organization, you are not recognized; you are anonymous. Going home from the job, going shopping or going to the cinema, nobody asks who you are. Walking in the streets of a city you take part in social life as a spectator among other spectators watching each other watch. The *flâneur* is a social innovation of the nineteenth century (see Featherstone, 1991: 72–5). A tourist is a twentieth-century *flâneur* (see Urry, 1990: 138). Their typical social environment is the semi-organized field. Tourists spend their time as passengers, customers, guests in hotels or visitors of museums.

Although it is not organized, interaction among unknown people is not disordered. There are rules and norms for such 'relations in public'. 'For example, a gallery goer can expect that when he is close to a picture, other patrons will make some effort to walk around his line of vision' (Goffman, 1971: 35). Forming queues in front of entrances is another norm of interaction among unknowns. Such norms, though, vary from place to place and have to be learnt by experience. You do what you see the others do.

Interaction in semi-organized fields may invite people into conversations with strangers. Passengers in a train or on a boat, guests in a restaurant or in a bar sometimes have opportunities to talk openly because of their anonymity and because they do not expect to meet again. Sexual dreams and fantasies often involve relations with unknown partners without commitments.

In interaction with unknown people nobody knows your past or your records. You are truly yourself. There are no commitments or promises or plans for the future involved. Nobody is going to ask you where you have been or what you have done or what you have achieved. Without an identity you are free. Identification is coercion.

Moving around outside organizations you meet people whom you have never seen before. When you do not recognize a person, traits such as age, sex, looks and skin colour acquire increased importance. In interaction outside organizations human actors display qualities that are neither organizational nor personal. Particularly in the way people dress they express, consciously or unconsciously, adherence to cultural norms, trends or fashions related to subculture, age group, sex, lifestyle or class position. Unlike wearing a uniform, you do not have to be admitted into or recognized by the subculture or lifestyle to wear clothes or a hairdo that identifies you with it. However, the way people dress is an important source of how they evaluate and judge each other when they have not met before, or when they do not know their organizational affiliations or positions. Foreigners or strangers such as tourists or immigrants are spotted through appearance and dress.

Cultural norms, rules and attitudes have their greatest importance outside organizations as a way of distinguishing people. Yet, such norms or signs are not without relation to organizational affiliation. They are often important for the selection of people into organizations.

Class is a common term for organizational imprints that distinguish people not on the ground of affiliations to particular organizations but according to organizational positions that are similar in many organizations of the same type; 'class consciousness is the projection of organizational statuses onto a larger political and economic canvas' (Stinch-combe, 1990: 308; cf. Baron, 1984). There are many ways to define social classes, but most of them build upon notions of relations within the realms of organizations such as control of employees or investments and relations to ownership (see Wright, 1985; Marshall et al., 1988; Blom et al., 1992).

Although the concept of class is derived from characteristics of organizational positions, it cuts across the existence of particular organizations. People affiliated with different organizations may belong to the same class, and people affiliated with the same organization may be in different classes. Members of the same family can belong to different classes (so-called cross-class families, see Leiulfsrud and Woodward, 1987). The actual class position of a person is a combination of several organizational affiliations such as family of origin, employment, education and present family. It is 'structured to a variable extent by mediated relations and temporal trajectories' (Wright, 1989: 347).

In order to explain income and standard of living within particular countries, class has been demonstrated throughout to have significant importance (Wright, 1985; Marshall et al., 1988). Class positions give rise to different lifestyles (see Weber, 1968: 305–7) with different cultural codes and norms as well as images of society. In this sense class positions are important sources of distinction among people outside organizations in ways of dress, speech, taste and manners (see Bourdieu, 1984). Class distinctions are used as typifications among unknown people.

Although relations between classes are derived from organizational contexts, classes are not necessarily turned into organizations. To become a class 'for itself' it has to be organized (see Marx, 1978: 160). The social power of classes has to be realized through class formation, that is, the constitution of class-based voluntary associations, typically unions or working-class parties.

## Networks

Recognition is a central aspect of human interaction. You behave differently towards a person that you know you have seen before than to a stranger. The implication of recognition is that you know something about a person, there is a history which simplifies further relations. You can talk about your previous encounter or about common friends or acquaintances. Recognition can be transferred through a third person. That is what happens when you are introduced to somebody.

Friendship is a form of recognition that is not organized. Relations of friendship evolve gradually (Porter and Tomaselli, 1989: 8). People rarely decide once and for all to become friends. There are no papers or contracts involved. Often you do not know if a friendship has ceased or not. In friendship relations there is no control or authority involved, and friends only rarely share collective resources. You do not ask a friend for permission. Claude Fischer (1982: 114) writes about 'the free-floating nature' of friendship. Thus, although friendship relations can involve several people, they are not organized (see Aldrich, 1979: 5).

Neither are friendship relations delimited in the same sense as affiliates of an organization. Nobody can really tell how many friends he or she has because one does not know. Friends are not counted. This is a problem for social science. It is hard to measure people's friendship ties (see Willmott, 1987; Garrett, 1989). There is a sliding scale of meaning between terms such as friends, mates and acquaintances, which indicates the gradual shifts in these relationships. According to one investigation conditions such as youth, childlessness and absence of nearby kin are positively correlated with the importance of friendship ties (Fischer, 1982: 117).

In social science literature friends, kin and perhaps neighbours of a person or a family are often regarded as networks. A network is based on personal relations and thus recognition, but a network must not be confused with an organization. There may be networks inside organizations or between different organizations. Networks rely more on the human parts than on the organizational parts of actions. There is a risk that the human parts will become too much involved. Affiliates of organizations are parts of larger networks stretching beyond the organizational context. People may spend their leisure time with colleagues and co-workers. Neighbours do not necessarily form networks, however. According to Fischer such ties are more 'residual than natural' (1982: 102).

To be affiliated with an organization is a different type of relationship than to be part of a network. Networks are complementary to organizations. We find it misleading to treat 'the world as a structure of networks', as some network theorists do (Wellman, 1988: 37–8). Sometimes the concept of network is used instead of, or as an alternative to, organization, because it gives connotations to personal relations between people rather than to bureaucracy and hierarchy, and it is perceived as more dynamic and creative.

Organizations are formalized units with distinct resources of power and methods of control that have a wider social significance than networks. In networks there are no methods for making collective decisions. There is no authority in networks. Their boundaries are floating. Of course, one can talk about affiliation to networks, although the process of exclusion is not as strong and sharp as in organizations. Networks have a tendency to 'ramify endlessly' (Knoke and Kuklinski, 1982: 24). In networks collective resources and power are not accumulated. They are rather relations of exchange of goods, help or information. Networks can be discussed in terms of density, reachability and centrality (Aldrich, 1986: 21). In this way networks are important for understanding what happens in interaction between organizations or to explain how people become affiliated with organizations, for instance, how they get jobs (Granovetter, 1973; Zucker, 1983: 30–3) or how they get married.

Networks can turn into organizations. The founding of organizations can often be understood in terms of network ties (see Granovetter, 1992: 8–9). This goes for firms as well as for voluntary associations. Thus, networks are important for the spread of organizations within and between countries (see chapter 7).

## Entries and exits

Steps from the outside to the inside of an organization are decisive moments in most people's lives, but you cannot choose your organizational affiliations. Either you are born into an affiliation, or you have to apply for admission. Often you can choose where to apply, but to be admitted you have to be selected, often among several other applicants. You have to fulfil certain requirements. This goes for getting a job, joining a party, or becoming a citizen of another state. It also holds true for marriage.

The ability to select new affiliates is one of the most

important aspects of organizational power. The power of organizations increases with the degree of people's dependence on organizational affiliation. On the other hand, organizations can be dependent upon supply of new affiliates. When there is a shortage of labour the power of firms is reduced. There is a constant interplay between organizations and people in their surroundings, where control of entries into organizations is a crucial moment.

To select new affiliates most organizations rely on previous organizational imprints of applicants, such as education, grades, class, previous work experience, political experience etc. Organizational recruiters often use their networks to get references of people. People are also selected because of sex, age, race, or appearance. Other ways of selecting new affiliates are through direct contacts with other organizations. People may be selected because of their other affiliations. One historically important example is the arranging of marriages between families. Organizations may also buy and sell affiliates between each other, as in the case of ice-hockey and soccer players.

Exit is another dimension of the switches between insides and outsides of organizations. In his well-known book *Exit, Voice and Loyalty*, Albert Hirschman (1970) discusses people's responses to decline in organizations. Possibilities to leave an organization are important power resources for affiliates. One restriction, however, is that exits often presuppose alternatives. People do not often leave a job without having a new job, although it happens (see Eriksson, 1991). To escape from a state you need to find another state that is willing to accept you as a new citizen. This is not the case, however, for most voluntary organizations or for marriages. Yet, leaving an organization is a big step. Many battered women still stay with their marriages, since 'the marital project is so highly valued' (Hydén, 1992: 152).

The discussion of entries into organizations is just as important as that of exits for an analysis of the interplay between people and organizations. Hirschman, however, hardly discussed entry at all. Power relations in processes of entry and exit stem from existing alternatives in terms of both organizations and people and the decisive factor is the ability of organizations to select their affiliates.

## Institutions and promotional culture

Boundaries of semi-organized fields are not as sharp as boundaries of organizations. Public relations, information and advertising are extensions of semi-organized fields in order to promote activities of an organization. 'Promotion crosses the line between advertising, packaging, and design, and is applicable as well, to activities beyond the immediately commercial' (Wernick, 1991: 181). Andrew Wernick regards promotion as a form of communication that 'is defined not by what it says but by what it does' (1991: 184). Fashion shows, press conferences, inaugurations are promotional events that are set up in cooperation with other organizations and, generally, with invited guests.

Semi-organized fields and promotions are not only arranged by firms; they are not only commercial. Parties arrange mass meetings and demonstrations where anybody can attend without any promises to come back and without being recognized. Charitable societies have their annual bazaars. Churches are open to anybody for watching ceremonies and services. To be baptized or married in the church, however, you have to be an affiliate. In their promotional activities members of voluntary organizations often use streets and squares to collect money or to distribute leaflets and propaganda.

In a state several semi-organized fields are constructed for promotional reasons. One type of activity is to create a national image by the construction of museums, memorials and monuments. One typical such item is the tomb of the Unknown Soldier (see Anderson, 1983: 17). Rituals and ceremonies to celebrate a national day are other examples of semi-organized fields of the state where everybody is invited.

The parliament is another semi-organized field of the state which is open to the public. Government meetings, however, take place behind closed doors.

Families are at times engaged in promotional activities. Weddings, for instance, are generally arranged in public. Anybody may come to the church or the place where the official wedding takes place to watch the ceremony and see the newly married couple. Weddings are advertised in newspapers as are other family events such as births and funerals.

Through promotional messages and activities, all types of organization attempt to master and regulate both organized and unorganized human activities. The result is a vast conglomeration of competing messages, products and ceremonies that often overlap and contradict each other. Boundaries between what is regarded as economy, politics, religion and arts are blurred. Organizations do not initiate all events on their outsides, but promotional activities of organizations to a large, and probably increasing, extent affect cultural and ideological processes: 'Promotion is a condition which has increasingly befallen discourses of all kinds; and the more it has done so, the more its modalities and relations have come to shape the formation of culture as a whole' (Wernick, 1991: 186). Wernick (1991: vii) suggests that it is this 'pan-promotionalism' that can account for many of the features of contemporary communications – intertextuality, de-referentiality, absorption of the real into its image' – that have been summarized under the term 'postmodern' (see Clegg, 1990: 17–20). The realm of postmodernism is outside organizations.

The distinction between insides and outsides of organizations is crucial. In the first chapter we emphasized the importance of distinguishing between organizations and institutions. In the 'new institutionalism' in organization theory this distinction is often blurred. This is not to say that the new institutionalism is all wrong. Its contribution is to put emphasis on phenomena such as cognitive models, taken-for-granted scripts, rules and classifications, or even myths, to explain the design of organizations (see DiMaggio and Powell, 1991a: 15). New firms, new parties or new families are created from concepts or ideas of how a certain type of organization should be constructed. Such concepts or ideas are summarized with the term 'institution', although the term is loose. It is not clear what shall count as institutions; whether, for example, ideologies or scientific knowledge should be included. We shall not try to define the term institution, only stress the point that institutions exist outside organizations. With the founding of a new organization, one or several institutional phenomena are turned into an organization with specific affiliates and collective resources. The mediator between institutions and organizations is often an entrepreneur, who connects institutional concepts with individuals into an organization. An entrepreneur can be a businessman, a missionary or an agitator: persons with ideas who look for people.

It is important to realize that most institutional phenomena are backed by or emanate from specific organizations. Many organizations, for instance states, universities, churches, parties, produce institutional messages consciously as part of their ongoing activities. Thus, institutions to a large extent can be understood as promotional culture.

Institutional phenomena can be taught in seminars, or learnt from reading books or journals, through going to exhibitions and shows or conferences. Institutional messages are also spread through participation, as Tocqueville (1961: 140) observed in the United States in the early nineteenth century: 'Political associations may therefore be considered as large free schools, where all the members of the community go to learn the general theory of association.'

After a time many promotional messages lose their particular organizational origin and become general cultural phenomena, such as religious or political ideas or a particular fashion. Other institutions cannot be comprehended without relating them to a particular organization, such as the laws of a state. Ideas and knowledge may also be protected by patent laws or copyright rules.

Even things that are not promoted, things that organizations try to keep secret, such as technology, methods of control or training, recipes, are spread because no organization has complete control of its affiliates. Eventually a few affiliates leave or escape and bring inside information with them. They carry the knowledge or information to the outside.

Old organizations encounter new institutional ideas and demands in the form of new laws, new managerial concepts, new political ideas, new products etc. The extent of the adaptation to new institutional demands or ideas varies between organizations. Some organizations that fail to adapt to new methods or demands may cease to exist; other organizations may adapt partly, or they may appear to adapt. This can be achieved through a decoupling of institutional and technical demands. Things may follow old routines inside the organization, but leaders or representatives of the organization say, and perhaps also believe, that everything has changed. Thus, there is an adapted facade, but activities go on as usual (Meyer and Rowan, 1991).

The distinction between institutions and ongoing organizational activities has been neglected in several contributions to the discussion of the new institutionalism. Many writers have regarded organizations as mere reflections of institutional societal sectors (Scott and Meyer, 1991: 122–5) or 'organizational fields' (DiMaggio and Powell, 1991b: 65). This tendency, however, has been criticized for regarding organizations as too passive and 'environments as overly constraining' (Powell, 1991: 194).

There is a continual interplay between organizations and institutions. Organizations produce institutions that later are used in the founding of new organizations. What is sometimes confusing is that many phenomena such as the family, various religions and ideas such as democracy or bureaucracy, simultaneously exist as organizations and as institutions (see Friedland and Alford, 1991: 249).

Laws can be understood as institutions. Criminal law is similar to control in semi-organized fields and distinct from rules inside organizations. If a person violates a criminal law, he or she can be punished, but nobody is rewarded for keeping the law, for waiting at red traffic lights or for not stealing. Criminal law pertains to everybody, not only to affiliates. People are punished as natural persons. In this sense the state is involved in arranging the order of semi-organized fields of other organizations, supermarkets, restaurants etc. These laws are prohibiting; they state what you must not do. Unlike rules in organizations, they do not say what you should do.

States also make laws to regulate other organizations, company law, labour law, family law, for instance. In these instances people are punished in their capacities as 'part organization'. A third kind of law pertains to citizens as affiliates and deals with citizens' rights, rights to vote, social insurances etc. Such laws also say what citizens should do – go to school or pay taxes, for instance. In relation to citizens of a particular state these laws are like internal organizational rules. In terms of relations between organizations these three kinds of law are different social phenomena.

## Summary: the realm of freedom?

Organization is about constructing certainty and control. To do this organizations recruit and select affiliates and collect resources. Organizations are enclosed, which does not imply that they do not care about their outsides. There are all sorts of ways for organizations to try to manage and influence what is going on outside their gates. But forms of control and influence are different on the outside. Outside their gates organizations cannot tell people what to do, only encourage them. To enhance exchange with the outside many organizations construct semi-organized fields, such as supermarkets, restaurants, theatres etc. From the perspective of the organization people in semi-organized fields are anonymous. People entering a semi-organized field are not selected by the organization, and customers, spectators or passengers do not have to come back. They do not even have to commit themselves to buy anything. Sometimes they will have to pay to enter. The most typical social figure of semi-organized fields is the tourist.

To lure people into their semi-organized fields organizations send messages. They engage in commercial and promotional activities to make their semi-organized fields known and attractive. Products, signs and events with an origin in organizations constitute a promotional culture which bombards outsides of organizations with films, books, newspapers, buildings, fashions, images, artefacts. Postmodern culture is an effect of increased emphasis in organizations on their outsides.

Interaction between unknown people in semi-organized fields is indirect. People watch each other, they do not cooperate. If people start to talk, for example, in a train or in a bar, it is an interaction without commitments. The people involved do not expect to see each other again. It is an interaction without a history or future, without control or expectations. In this sense the semi-organized field is a realm of freedom.

Passing each other in semi-organized fields people are neither representatives of organizations nor individuals. It is here that signs of distinction, such as dress and hairstyle, related to age, gender, class, lifestyle, or subculture, have the greatest significance.

You do not have to be affiliated with an organization to be recognized. Not all human interaction is organized. Friendship is not. Friends do not control each other, and friends do not make decisions to become friends. Friendship just happens and develops gradually. Relations between friends are more freefloating than relations between affiliates of the same organization (although they can also be friends outside the organizational context). There are not only your friends, there are also the friends of your friends and their friends. Relationships of friendship and acquaintances are often described as networks. Networks are not organized, but they can turn into organizations. Networks are important for recruitment of people to new as well as existing organizations.

Steps between insides and outsides of organizations are crucial events in most people's lives. Becoming affiliated with or leaving an organization is often a dramatic event that you remember all your life. Changes of affiliations, such as getting a new job or being divorced, determine the routines of everyday life for a long time.

Although organizations are the predominating figurations in the social landscape, their control is far from complete. Organizations cannot control how their products are used. When people talk or think about messages, ideas, knowledge produced by organizations these phenomena lose their connection with their origin. People use products of organizations at their own discretion. The way people talk, read and think about what is going on in the social landscape does not follow organizational rules. New values and new demands are generated in interaction outside organizations. In order to have a lasting impact in the social landscape, however, new values and ideas have to be moulded into organized forms.

# 5

# INSIDE ORGANIZATIONS

## Fragile wholes and recalcitrant parts

One cannot understand human action without relating it to an organizational context. To understand organizations, on the other hand, one has to consider the human actors. But organizations are not only made up of affiliates. Organizations keep resources related to their goals and purposes. There are rules, a constitution, and common knowledge. Human actions are filtered into an organizational coordination via positions.

The power of an organization *vis-à-vis* affiliates is derived from their interest in the organization and the rights all affiliates have in relation to its resources. That is the power of authority. The most obvious sign of the organizational totality is its performance, for example, the music played by an orchestra, or for that matter the music played on CDs or tapes produced by a record company, the political performance of a party, the results of a football game, the sales figures of a shop.

The connection of organizational resources, rules and positions with individual affiliates is not easily achieved, however. The fit between the whole and its parts is rarely perfect, and a certain slack is normal in any organization (Scott, 1992: 235). An organization can hardly survive if peak performances are required all the time. But there cannot be too much slack either, or the organization is in danger of dissolution. And many organizations do fail (see Barnard, 1968: 5).

In organizations human actions are combined with technological devices. Most organizations apply methods of technology to decrease dependence on unpredictable human parts. Machines are not totally predictable either, but they are usually easier to control than human beings. The level of performance can be increased through the use of technology: speed, force, precision, endurance. Most obviously this is the case in the organization of production, but through computer based technology this is increasingly done in administration, information and services. Services are automated through, for instance, banking machines or answering machines. In a broader perspective public relations and relations to audiences are transferred into technological relations. Books, journals, tapes, films, videos, replace human actors as representatives of organizations. Orchestras and theatre ensembles have been replaced by recorded products. But all human action cannot be replaced. Organizations are no machines.

Imagine a machine where some of the parts walk away every evening or whenever it stops operating, only to come back, when it will start again. And while they are away they may change. An organization is a puzzle that has to be put together again and again. Its human parts cannot be glued or screwed together once and for all. Nor can they be inscribed into a microchip as integrated circuits.

Since the parts of an organization are not fixed together once and for all there is a fragility in all organizational constructions. The reiterated assembling of parts can be understood in relations between the dependence of affiliates on an organization and their dependence on other organizations or people in the surrounding social landscape where they spend some of their time. How an organization is fitted together can thus be seen in the tension between centripetal forces within the organization and centrifugal forces in the environment. However, there may also be centripetal forces at work outside an organization that contribute to its stability.

The mutual dependence of all affiliates on each other yields a general power inside an organization that contributes to its stability. The extent to which affiliates of an organization depend on resources of one or several particular affiliates contributes to its fragility.

## Power inside organizations: authority and influence

When you become affiliated with an organization you leave some of the control of your behaviour to the other affiliates, that is, you yield the control of particular aspects of your behaviour to the authority of the organization. In exchange for losing some of your self-determination you get access to resources. You acquire at least some rights, however limited they may be. Authority is derived from the collective effort of an organizaton. The power of authority has to be backed by monitoring and sanctioning capacities.

The authority of an organization is related to actions on its behalf, and it is only applicable to affiliates of the same organization (Barnard, 1968: 173). It is based on the fact that all affiliates have at least some interest in what the organization is doing, and thus it is an expression of the awareness 'that what is at stake is the good of the organization' (Barnard, 1968: 171).

In common perception organizations are associated with terms such as hierarchy and bureaucracy. But authority is more fundamental to organizations than either hierarchy or bureaucracy. There are organizations with no hierarchy or bureaucracy, but there are no organizations without authority. It is a mistake to regard authority as intrinsically coming from the top of the organization, even though in practice it often does. Anybody requesting anything or controlling anything in the name or interest of the organization does this as an expression of the common authority of all affiliates who depend on the performance of the organization. Authority is generated through the interdependence of all affiliates. In an organization with a democratic form of decision-making, anybody can speak in the name of decisions taken in common meetings, referring to it as 'this is what we agreed upon'. That is speaking in the name of the authority of the organization.

Chester Barnard in his book *The Functions of the Executive* puts much stress on the executive as the one symbolizing authority. But he emphasizes that there is a personal interest among all affiliates in the maintenance of authority, which is largely a function of informal organization. 'Its expression goes under the name of "public opinion", "organization opinion", "feeling in the ranks", "group attitude", etc.' (1968: 169). Only after this general statement does he talk about 'the fiction that authority comes down from above' (1968: 170).

The process of acquiring and securing authority and legitimacy is more complicated in organizations with compulsory affiliation, since in such organizations the yielding of authority is not a deliberate choice that comes with the acceptance of an affiliation. It has to be induced through upbringing, education etc. Since organizations with compulsory affiliation (states, families) cannot dismiss affiliates who do not accept the authority, these types of organization have practised harsher forms of coercion than organizations with voluntary affiliation.

Authority is first of all about tasks and performances on behalf of an organization. Authority is about what people can be ordered to do in their capacities as affiliates with certain positions. And as affiliates they have accepted control over some but not all of their actions. Actions that an affiliate expects to be within the control of the organization can be said to lie within 'the zone of indifference' (Barnard, 1968: 169; Simon, 1991: 31). Bacharach and Lawler (1980: 38) talk about the scope of authority.

As an employee of an enterprise you accept to obey orders on what to do on the job, but in many jobs you do not accept orders about how to dress. In other jobs, dress and speech may be within the zone of indifference, that is, an employee is prepared to obey orders on what clothes to wear on the job. Female secretaries may accept orders about making coffee, but male clerks in the same office would probably not. The range of the zone of indifference varies between jobs and from organization to organization. All types of affiliation imply a zone of indifference, and the zone of indifference can be more or less contested. This goes for citizenship as well as family membership.

From the notion of a zone of indifference follows that authority finally rests upon the acceptance of each individual (see Barnard, 1968: 163). Even if authority as such cannot be contested as long as you belong to the organization, the particular range of the zone of indifference may be contested, and its limits may change. 'The zone of indifference will be wider or narrower depending upon the degree to which the inducements exceed the burdens and sacrifices which determine the individual's adhesion to the organization' (Barnard, 1968: 169).

Although everybody has accepted the authority this does not mean that all are equally content or loyal. After some time individual affiliates may redefine their situation and wish to change it without abandoning the organization. The possibilities and the power different affiliates have to change the organization according to their particular interests has been referred to as influence. Influence is related to how much the organization depends on each particular affiliate either in terms of his or her position or his or her personal qualities.

It is important to treat authority and influence as 'distinctly different dimensions' of power within organizations (Bacharach and Lawler, 1980: 27–9). Several writers regard authority as one source of power among others (see for instance Mintzberg, 1983: 5), and Pfeffer (1981: 4–5) talks about the transformation of power into authority. But authority is there from the beginning. It stems from the organization as a totality, whereas influence stems from its parts. One problem is that the power of authority can be mixed with power of influence. Individuals executing authority may use their position to gain influence.

After an extensive discussion of several approaches to sources of power in terms of influence, Bacharach and Lawler (1980: 35–7) distinguish three such sources: expertise, opportunity and personality. Mintzberg (1983: 24) makes similar distinctions.

## Centripetal and centrifugal forces

Organizations are formed under tensions between centripetal and centrifugal forces that keep affiliates together or make them drift apart. The stronger the centripetal forces the stronger the cohesion in the organization. It is due to centripetal forces that people do come back. If centrifugal forces get the upper hand the organization is likely to dissolve. The particular shape of an organization is contingent on the combination of many sources of centripetal and centrifugal forces. The design of positions and their coordination have to be adjusted to local preconditions. In their contingency organization theory Lawrence and Lorsch stated: 'Internal attributes of the organization, in terms of structure and orientation, can be tested for goodness of fit with the various environmental variables and the predispositions of members' (1986: 209).

One centripetal force of the organization is its amount of resources. Larger resources generate stronger centripetal forces, because costs are higher to leave a resourceful organization. The resources of an organization are related to the dependence of individual affiliates of the organization. A heart surgeon, for instance, is more dependent on a resourceful organization than a psychiatrist. It is a greater step for a politician to leave a powerful party than to leave a party without any political impact. The strength of the centripetal force of large resources is also due to the existence of alternatives – in the case of a politician, an alternative party. The status of an organization can be viewed as part of its resources. The prestige of being affiliated to a certain organization is a centripetal force.

Coercive aspects of organizations are centripetal forces related to possibilities of monitoring and sanctioning. Sanctioning capacities rely on resources, both in order to reward and to punish. Organizations have to concentrate on things it is possible to control. Experts are harder to control than operators, which is one reason why consultants are used for doing expert jobs. It is easier to control people who are expected to do the same thing day after day (routine work); that is why the stable and homogeneous environment of an organization can be said to constitute a centripetal force contributing to the persistence and cohesion of organizations.

Satisfaction of affiliates with what they do for an organization and what they get out of it is an important centripetal force, as well as loyalty and a strong commitment. An ideological commitment towards the goals of an organization also works centripetally. Strong ties of affection and a feeling of closeness within the organization are other centripetal forces.

An important centripetal force from the outside is a strong institutional or monetary support from another organization. Such support can keep organizations going even without a high level of commitment from affiliates and even without much control or sanctioning capacity. An example of such an organization could be a school in an area of a city with many poor and single-parent families, where neither parents nor children care much about the school, and where there is a high turnover of teachers or perhaps teachers with inadequate training. In such a situation the organization survives only because of institutional support (for examples and a discussion of 'permanently failing organizations' see Meyer and Zucker, 1989).

Some organizations are pushed together from the outside by customers, passengers, or clients, who check the activities of affiliates, particularly in semi-organized fields, in order to get their service.

The balance between centripetal and centrifugal forces can operate more freely in organizations with voluntary affiliation. Chances are greater that affiliates who do not fit in, and obstruct coordination, can disappear from the organization. This enhances centripetal forces in organizations with voluntary affiliation. On the other hand, organizations with compulsory affiliation cannot be entirely dissolved, although states can be divided into smaller states. But the largest problem for organizations with compulsory affiliation, that is, kinship and citizenship, is not to avoid being dissolved, but to create a cohesion and legitimate solidarity without being able to select their affiliates or get rid of some of them.

In organizations with few common resources, a weak internal culture, unclear aims and low monitoring and sanctioning capacities, centrifugal forces can be strong and make for the dissolution of the organization. This is often the situation in newly created organizations and may account for the 'liability of newness' (Stinchcombe, 1965: 148).

Artisans such as painters, goldsmiths or hairdressers often work on their own or in small organizations. They do not depend on large resources to be able to do their jobs. The fragility of knowledge based enterprises, in computing, for instance, can be attributed to the few common resources. Centrifugal forces are strong when people in an organization do not depend on others to do their tasks.

For individual affiliates there is a varying but nearly always present centrifugal force in the wish for control of one's own behaviour and a wish for self-determination. Even though people choose to cooperate they do not always like to do it, at least not every day or every time.

When there are alternative organizational affiliations available out there, such as many jobs or many churches, strong centrifugal forces are working that must be balanced by loyalty, routine, or rewards. Multiple affiliations and strong network ties outside the organization may be momentous centrifugal forces, leading to interaction such as corruption or nepotism weakening the cohesion and coordination of organized activities. A heterogeneous and changing environment leads to more specialized and more varied positions within the organization, which may weaken the coordination if the organizational culture is not strong enough.

Most conditions that make up centripetal forces are at the same time conditions that account for inertia and inflexibility. Strong networks within the organization, traditional routines, satisfied affiliates and a strong culture prevent adjustments – towards a changing environment – in the way things are done. This is the reason why organizations by necessity are inert (see Aldrich, 1992: 28–9). Adjustments are possible, but the balance between centripetal and centrifugal forces is difficult to establish and even more so to maintain.

## Positions

Organizations are often visualized as pyramids, even though some are flatter than others, with a concentration of authority and knowledge at the top. In organizational charts the building blocks of an organization are not fixed together as the stones of a pyramid. They are only connected through arrows. This part of the analysis of the inside of an organization deals with its building blocks, that is, with organizational positions. The next section deals with the arrows, how the building blocks are made to fit together, that is, the inner logic of an organization. Although it will be obvious that it is not quite possible to discuss these two aspects separately, we believe there are good reasons for trying to do so. The final section will deal with incentives to cooperate and the centrifugal force of influence.

Social processes of differentiation take place inside organizations. Both the division of labour and the class structure emanate from within organizations. Division of labour is first of all an intraorganizational process (Clegg, 1990: 10).

If class is seen as caused by subordination in work, it is a phenomenon that must be understood in its organizational context, particularly in terms of employment. The unequal distribution of power within an organization generates contradictions. Yet, the mutual dependence of affiliates of an organization encourages the common interests of all affiliates and is thus a centripetal force that may overshadow contradictions of a class character.

Positions in organizations are constructed to fit individuals. The idea of a position is that it should be 'filled' with a recognized person. Positional actions are everyday routines. Most people live their everyday life in the realm of one or several organizational positions. Organizational positions determine what people do and their opportunity structures.

Positions within organizations can first of all be described in terms of degrees of specialization and authority (see Littler, 1982: 42), that is, what tasks should be done and what power comes with the position. Positions are the filters that separate actions on behalf of organizations from other aspects of actions.

Specialization is often described as the amount of qualification or knowledge that is required to fulfil the tasks of a position. There are processes of both requalification and dequalification going on, implying that people need more or fewer qualifications to fulfil their tasks. Positions can be more or less standardized. There is also a horizontal specialization (Mintzberg, 1979: 69–71), which is not described in terms of how much you have to know, but in terms of what you know – a craft or expertise knowledge, or a profession such as doctor or teacher, for example.

Both authority and specialization are contested concepts, since they suppress the freedom and creativity of human action. Is it possible to have lasting organizations without authority and without specialization, that is, without specific positions? To our knowledge there is little empirical evidence to support such a view. All experience seems to support the view that in 'groups' or organizations that start out to function without either authority or specialization, after some time an informal structure evolves. In a discussion of feminist grass-roots organizations it is reported: 'Our experience as grass-roots activists is that no matter how much we tried to structure our organization in ways that eliminated leadership, it did not disappear, and its unacknowledged existence was a constant source of tension' (Adamson et al., 1988: 238). This is not to say that organizations cannot be democratic, only that a recognized distribution of authority is an intrinsic quality of all organizations. Specialization, on the other hand, is not fundamental in the same sense, although it is almost always there.

The terminology to distinguish between positions varies between different forms of organization – in an army, in a church, in a university, in a football club, or in a family. Descriptions of positions can be more or less general. In a specific industry one can distinguish several positions for workers, but when comparing different industries you often only separate blue-collar and white-collar workers, for instance. And similar organizations, in terms of skills and occupations, often differ significantly in the way they describe and label positions (see Baron and Bielby, 1986).

One method of summarizing types of position has been suggested by Henry Mintzberg (1979). He distinguishes between five basic parts, corresponding to special positions, in organizations: operating core, middle line, strategic apex, technostructure and support staff. He then outlines five typical constellations of positions into five pure types of organizations: simple structure, machine bureaucracy, professional bureaucracy, divisionalized form and adhocracy. Pure types, however, are rarely found. Most existing organizations are hybrids between two or several pure types (Mintzberg, 1979: 474–7). The reason is that organizations cannot be constructed from blueprints like machines or cars. An organization is never complete. It has to be constructed continuously and be adjusted to the outside. The shape of positions is contingent on processes surrounding the organization, but at the same time they have to fit reasonably well together. An actual form is the result of tensions between centrifugal and centripetal forces. Any good solution of an organizational problem is only occasional.

Below we will discuss four main conditions outside an

organization that are essential for determining the shape of positions: supply and qualifications of individuals, technology, institutional processes and concepts and, finally, the general environment or constellation of significant organizations.

## Supply of individuals

All kinds of human action and abilities can be used in organizations, but not at the same time in the same position. Bodily attributes as well as special knowledge or skill may be equally important. Positions can be designed to use only a few human qualities or to use a broad range of human attributes. In the former case the dependence of the organization on specific individuals is weak, and in the latter case it is strong.

In a general sense qualities and attributes of people available to an organization to a substantial degree determine design of positions. Being available here means either that they have time for the required organizational activities, or that they can be attracted from other organizations. But, as Arthur Stinchcombe has pointed out, the stronger the centripetal forces in existing organizations, 'the tougher the job of establishing a new organization' (1965: 150).

In a broad perspective literacy is a necessary requirement for several modern forms of bureaucratic organization or for voluntary associations: 'Men cannot easily start their own Christian sect unless someone can read the Scriptures' (Stinchcombe, 1965: 150).

Taylorism is an extreme form of specialization of positions in manufacturing that implies a 'minimum relationship' between organization and individual (see Littler, 1982: 160). Taylorism can be understood as an adjustment to the supply of people willing to take jobs in industries in the United States at the beginning of the twentieth century. A relative lack of skilled workers in combination with extensive immigration was a background for the design of extremely specialized positions, which could be filled with almost anybody. Taylorism increased the substitutability of affili-ates. 'The shortages of craftsmen led to high wages for skilled workers, which in turn led to an increasing division of labour according to skill' (Littler, 1982: 176). In Japan the supply of individuals available for the early industrialization was very different. It was difficult to recruit people to the new industries, and people were not willing to take up paid employment (Littler; 1982: 148; cf. Lincoln and Kalleberg, 1990: 22). The early ad hoc strategies of Japanese employers in order to decrease labour turnover and to get better trained workers were to create centripetal forces through, for instance, a factory dormitory system and a contract system, *oyakata*, simulating kinship ties (Littler, 1982: 149–52). Even-tually this led to the now well-known Japanese corporate welfare system.

Existence of alternative affiliations is a strong centrifugal force against organizational effort. Exits from relations of employment are easier to accomplish when there are many jobs available. When unemployment is low people have more choices and alternatives to look for better jobs. In such a situation enterprises, in order to attract and make people come back, have to design positions that are more satisfac-tory. One method, of course, is to increase wages, but jobs (positions) also have to be more attractive. This centrifugal force can explain why Volvo plants in Sweden in the 1980s were forced to upgrade assembly work, whereas car manu-facturers in, for instance, England, with a lower labour turnover and higher unemployment, had no need for this strategy (see Pontusson, 1990; Sandberg et al., 1992: 301–3). In general, there is evidence to suggest that high labour turnover (many exits and entries) has several effects on business organizations, for instance, more administration and formalization but also more innovation. It seems, however, to decrease productivity (see Price, 1989).

Most voluntary associations grew in new cities or commu-nities where people had time to spend outside the realm of the family and away from work. Voluntary associations were designed for the participation of members. McCarthy and

Zald (1987b), however, have noticed a recent trend in the design of positions in new 'professional social movements'. Instead of participating in the activities of the organization, members pay high membership fees and the organizational activities are run by specialized employees or professionals. Members' lack of time to devote to the organization means the positions in the organization become professionalized.

## Technology

The impact of technology varies with the type of activity that an organization is involved in, but also within the same type of activity the adjustment between individuals and technology (capital/labour ratio, see Aldrich and Mueller, 1982) is not completely obvious. Most empirical research on relations between level of technology and positions in organizations has confirmed the importance of technology although the relationship is 'relatively weak' (Scott, 1992: 241).

In a broad historical perspective, however, the development of technology has had a decisive influence on the design of positions in all organizations: in the family, in the army, in parties and churches but probably most of all in business enterprises.

During the late 1950s and 1960s much of the research on organizations was concentrated on the relationship between technology and structure. One of the most cited investigations was one by Joan Woodward (1965). Her results were summarized into a distinction between three types of technology – unit production, mass production and process production – with distinctive organizational consequences. Mass production was found to lead to the lowest levels of skill formation and the highest degrees of standardization and control in positions (Woodward, 1965: 64–6). The idea of three levels of production technology can be found in several other works, for instance Robert Blauner's (1964) book on the labour process, *Alienation and Freedom*, and Richard Edwards's (1979) discussion of changing forms of control.

Although there are clear technological imperatives there are also alternatives. If there are people around who can be induced to work for low wages the most advanced technology may not be very rational for an investor.

## Institutional processes

In chapter 4 we discussed the interplay between organizations and institutions. Whereas organizations are relatively easy to define and recognize, it is harder to recognize institutional processes, but they are important in order to understand design of positions. According to Scott (1992: 132), institutional processes are 'characterized by the elaboration of rules and requirements'. Such rules and requirements may appear in many forms, for instance, laws, knowledge, taken-for-granted notions, public opinion, or may come from specific demands from significant other organizations, for instance professional organizations or unions. In relation to positions, institutional demands may either prohibit a certain design of positions or make specific requirements about what aspects a certain position should contain. Laws against child labour, for instance, affect the possible design of positions in many organizations. In many typical voluntary associations there are traditional norms for positions in an elected executive (president, vice-president, secretary, treasurer). These norms are often spread through handbooks (Adamson et al., 1988: 231).

Meyer and Scott distinguish some types of organization that are heavily restricted in their design by both institutional and technical demands, such as banks, utilities and general hospitals. Examples of organizations encountering strong institutional demands, but weaker technical demands, are churches and schools. As examples of organizations with few institutional demands they mention restaurants and health clubs (see Scott and Meyer, 1991: 123–6; Scott, 1992: 133).

DiMaggio and Powell (1991b: 67) have identified three processes through which institutional processes occur: coercive isomorphism, mimetic isomorphism and normative isomorphism. In a case of mimetic isomorphism, that is to say, imitation, representatives of an organization try to imitate forms from other organizations which they perceive as successful, although this does not imply 'that the most important organizational problems are being solved' (Fligstein, 1985: 388). Isomorphism often occurs independently of whether the particular organizational form improves efficiency or not.

Families as organizations are heavily influenced by institutional processes both from states and from cultural norms. These demands, however, do not always determine the development of the organization of families. New forms of unmarried cohabitation evolved contrary to institutional demands. Institutional expectations concerning the division of labour in a family may be turned upside down due to other organizational affiliations of spouses. For instance, in families where the wife has the highest paid and most qualified job the divison of labour in the household may diverge substantially from expected norms (see Leiulfsrud and Woodward, 1987).

## Shifting environments

Environment is a concept that has been widely used in organization theory. In a general sense environment means all that creates uncertainty for an organization. As has been emphasized earlier, much of what has been discussed as 'environments' is in fact other organizations (see Aldrich and Mueller, 1982: 40). But there are also individuals and institutions in the environment. The environment of an organization is the social landscape, or it can be comprehended in terms of constellations of organizations, which we will discuss more in the two following chapters. Here we will present some of the arguments and findings of organization theorists of the 1960s, who analysed environments in terms of their degree of uncertainty, that is, their degrees of homogeneity and stability. Much of the uncertainty was related to the marketing of products.

In an investigation of twenty industrial companies in Scotland in the 1950s Burns and Stalker found two divergent forms of organization. One they called 'mechanistic' and the other 'organic'. In the mechanistic form positions were specialized and differentiated according to functional tasks with precise definitions of rights and obligations attached to each functional role. There was also a concentration of knowledge at the top of the pyramid. In the organic form there was a continual redefinition of the content of positions, and positions were designed according to special knowledge (a horizontal specialization) (Burns and Stalker, 1961: 119–22). The explanation for these differences was to be found in the environment of the enterprises. The mechanistic form was typical of firms in a stable technical environment with a stable market, whereas organic forms were typical of businesses surviving under unstable business conditions. Thompson (1967: 72–3) presents similar arguments about relations between organizations in homo- and heterogeneous environments that are either stable or shifting.

The organizational form that Burns and Stalker called organic has been discussed and analysed by Mintzberg (1979: 431ff.) as an 'adhocracy'. The same formal elements have been labelled postindustrial or postmodern organizations. Typically, in an adhocracy the division of labour is informal and flexible. Such an organization is often small, and its activities are often in service and information and it is technologically advanced (see Heydebrand, 1989: 327).

When the definition of positions is looser and more flexible an organization becomes more dependent on the individual occupying a position, which calls for changing methods of coordination and control. Burns and Stalker emphasized the importance in 'organic' organizations of a total commitment to organizational objectives from individual employees. As Gordon Marshall (1990: 99) has pointed out, this finding was an anticipation of much of what has been emphasized in the management literature during the 1980s.

## Coordination between positions

If constraints and demands from the outside totally determined positions in an organization, it would probably not last very long. Positions have to be fitted together into a working unit in order to counteract centrifugal forces. Even if the fit between positions is rarely perfect, centripetal forces are developed to balance the influence from the surrounding social landscape. But all forms of organization are not possible everywhere. The range of feasible organizational forms in a particular area of the social landscape is restricted. That is why some organizations move rather than try to adjust, and many more organizations fail. Organizations can also change conditions on the outside, for instance, in influencing lawmaking or public opinion, to enable them to have more control of their design of positions. Organizations can to some extent, under certain conditions, create their own environment (see Pfeffer and Salancik, 1978).

Sometimes it is possible to change relations between positions without a concomitant change in the environment. What is required is a new idea of how to do things. A new coach with new ideas may change the strategy of a soccer team from one season to another without replacing any of the players. Peterson has studied how in one Swedish team it was possible to change the definition of each player's role on the field and the relations between different parts of the team through a standardization of what was expected of each player and an increased interdependence and coordination between offensive and defensive players, with remarkable results (1993: 147–8).

Such success in changing the inner logic of organizations is unusual, however. How to improve coordination between positions, that is, the inner logic of an organization, is one of the major tasks of much research on organizations. But it is easier to change the blueprints or charts of organizations than to change what people are really doing, because of constraints from the outside. Proposals to change organizations from within are often only wishful thinking.

The inner logic between positions is to a large extent due to the nature of interdependence of tasks. The interdependence of the musicians and the conductor in a symphony orchestra is different from the interdependence of pupils and teachers in a class. Even though time and presence are important in a school they are more important in a symphony orchestra. Interdependence can be described along several dimensions, and the nature of the interdependence affects the coordination between positions. It is one thing to coordinate people who do the same thing at the same place at the same time and another to coordinate people who do different things at different places on different occasions, for instance, researchers in a sociology department. Interdependence can also be related to which parts of a product need to be made first, or whether different parts have to be manufactured or developed simultaneously (Thompson, 1967: 54–5).

Weber's theory of bureaucracy (1968: 956–65) is above all a theory about coordination between positions. Key elements of bureaucratic mechanisms are the stress on hierarchy and on general rules. To achieve predictable results and to make any planning possible in large organizations, decisions and orders have to follow a hierarchical structure. Rules are mechanisms that say how actions from different positions are to be fitted together; they say what has to be done first, and which positions do certain tasks. Rules facilitate coordination within an organization, but they may also make an organization less flexible (Perrow, 1986: 20–6).

Bureaucracy is not a special form of organization. Bureaucratic elements may exist to different degrees and in different combinations in many forms of organization. Marshall Meyer (1985: 25–6) pointed out that the preconditions for bureaucratic growth are different in business enterprises from those in most state agencies. State agencies are generally more exposed to institutional demands from other organizations, but they are also less flexible. They cannot be closed or moved as easily as business enterprises, and thus their organizational structure is less likely to be radically changed.

Often state agencies follow a 'problem-organization-problem-more organization cycle' (Meyer, 1985: 179).

Depending on the nature of the interdependence different positions require shifting amounts and kinds of information, and the need for information-processing is related to the overall structure of the organization. When the need for information is comparatively low a hierarchical structure is not useful, but when it increases, that is, when the degree of interdependence is higher, a hierarchical organization of positions may be appropriate, since it reduces transmission costs of information. The relationship between information needs and hierarchy seems to be curvilinear. When the need for information continues to increase, hierarchies become overloaded and a decentralized structure may be more useful (see Scott, 1992: 161; cf. Woodward, 1965: 67).

Another method of decreasing the need for information-processing is a standardization of positions. The more positions are standardized, the less is the need for a continuous flow of new information. Standardization reduces the problem of coordination and allows for larger work units and wider spans of control (Mintzberg, 1979: 139). When and if standardization of positions is unfeasible, for instance, due to a heterogeneous environment, the problem of coordination increases. Adhocracies have high costs of communication to accomplish their mutual adjustment; 'people talk a lot in these structures' (Mintzberg, 1979: 463). Similarly, in families, the less standardized the positions of the spouses, the more they have to talk to each other and to transmit information about what to buy for dinner and who is to take the children to school or to their swimming classes.

There are often tensions between institutional demands from the outside and the inner logic of coordination. If an organization depends on isomorphism with institutionalized rules, and these rules to some extent are incompatible with practical requirements for organized activities, the formal structure may become decoupled from what individual affiliates do. This allows an organization to maintain a formal structure that is contrary to what is really going on.

Decoupling implies that the inspection and control of the performance is minimized or results are made invisble or ignored, and goals are made ambiguous (Meyer and Rowan, 1991: 57–8). In the same way families may handle demands from authorities or relatives by presenting a facade at anniversaries or on other occasions, which is quite different from what goes on inside the family.

Although the notion of decoupling or loose coupling is against common sense expectations of organized actions, such couplings are none the less often necessary, since the tension between outer constraints and demands and the inner logic is strong. If it were not for a loose coupling there would be occasional 'normal accidents' in all complex systems of interdependence.

Complex interdependence is due to the existence of interconnected subsystems within an organization and an absence of spatial segregation of activities, that is to say, proximity. The interdependence of positions is greater in complex systems than in linear systems, partly due to the nature of tasks and to technology. Among linear organizations, in this sense, there are assembly line production processes and post offices, and among complex organizations, nuclear plants and universities. The difference between universities and nuclear plants in terms of coordination is that universities are loosely coupled whereas nuclear plants are tightly coupled. Loose coupling means that there are alternative methods available to do things and that processing delays are possible (Perrow, 1984: 96–8). 'If interactive complexity and tight coupling – system characteristics – inevitably will produce an accident, I believe we are justified in calling it a *normal accident*' (Perrow, 1984: 5).

In many voluntary associations there is a contradiction in the inner logic between the democratic constitution, the rights of all members to decide about the activities of the organization, and the need for quick decisions and actions in, for instance, a political struggle. The need for speedy decisions and the need for specialists in a hostile environment necessarily cause a problem of coordination between the democratic decision-making procedures and the tasks of the executive. Thus Robert Michels (1962: 70) claimed in his book *Political Parties*: 'Organization implies the tendency to oligarchy.' Oligarchy, for Michels, does not necessarily imply that employed functionaries use their influence to promote their own interests, only that they have to take action independently of the official constitution, which may be too slow in a changing and hostile environment.

## Individuals, influence and incentives

Even if positions are to a substantial extent designed to fit individuals given their alternatives and constraints, there is nearly always a dual involvement. Even if people have joined an organization voluntarily, either as an employee or as a member or through marriage, it is one thing to make commitments to be accepted as an affiliate and another thing to come back time and again. Enthusiasm and motivation may be deteriorating (see Silverman, 1971: 212–13), at the same time as alternatives and possibilities to exit become fewer. Organizations may become traps.

Even though people join an organization to be able to take advantage of its resources one must count upon the fact that there is a discrepancy between what affiliates want to do and what they should do as part of the organization. Barnard concludes that 'unless an individual can be induced to cooperate there can be no cooperation' (1968: 139, see also pp. 88–9).

The problem of making people cooperate is greatest in cases of compulsory affiliation, and when people cannot easily be excluded, which explains the existence of coercion and violence in states and in families. In voluntary associations the issue of inducing affiliates to cooperate can be expected to be less critical than in other forms of organization, since voluntary associations presuppose some value consensus, although this is not to say the problem does not exist also in voluntary associations.

Incentives or rewards are central in achieving cooperation. There is also persuasion. Barnard (1968: 142) makes a distinction between several kinds of incentive, such as: money or other material rewards, prestige, distinction, desirable physical conditions of work, conformity to habitual practices, satisfaction of personal ideals, the feeling of enlarged participation, the condition of communion.

Incentives are usually offered in combinations. In the case of employment, however, wages or other forms of monetary rewards are the most important incentives. Among wage forms the piece rate system most clearly connects monetary rewards to individual performance. Too large differences in pay, however, may create incentives for affiliates to be uncooperative, and thus contribute to a lower general performance of the organization. Pay compression improves incentives for cooperation among workers (see Lazear, 1991). When it is difficult to observe the direct output from an individual employee, it has been argued that an 'upward-sloping wage-earnings profile' (Lazear, 1991) is a way to create incentives to come back and stay with an organization. The same idea was part of Weber's (1968) characteristics of a bureaucratic mode of organization, namely a career within the bureaucratic hierarchy. The same principle, to offer affiliates better conditions according to their time in the organization, is also discussed as career management (see Herriot, 1992) or firm internal labour markets (see Lincoln and Kalleberg, 1990: 15; cf. Burawoy, 1979: 95–108). A career within the hierarchy of an organization does not only imply higher wages, it usually also means increased prestige and improved working conditions. In a family there is a natural career in terms of the right for children to inherit their parents. Preconditions for careers in families have varied between siblings depending upon age and sex due to differences in rules. All princes do not become kings.

In voluntary associations incentives such as satisfaction of personal ideals, the feeling of participation and what Barnard called the condition of communion, or what Etzioni (1961: 5) called symbolic rewards, are more significant. These incentives, however, are often also there in relation to employment in business enterprises or in state agencies. Conversely, there are sometimes good reasons for turning some members of voluntary associations into employees and giving them monetary rewards apart from the symbolic rewards that are prevalent in such organizations (see Michels, 1962: 135–40).

Incentives are related to individual affiliates and are at least indirectly based on their performance. A reward follows after a performance, and it presupposes individual control. When control of individual performance is difficult or unfeasible because of the nature of the tasks, or because it is impossible to monitor, other inducements are required. Mintzberg (1979: 98) talks about indoctrination in cases 'where jobs are sensitive or remote'. As examples he mentions managers of a foreign subsidiary or ambassadors of a state. When monitoring is difficult, socialization of affiliates becomes all the more important. Since the early 1980s much attention has been paid in research on organizations to the cultural aspects of organizations as a response to research that questioned the impact of formal steering mechanisms. This research on organizational culture was thus aimed at using culture as 'the basis for organizational rationality' (Ouchi and Wilkins, 1985: 468–9) and to 'counteract the centrifugal tendencies of decentralization and loose coupling' (Heydebrand, 1989: 347). However, many of these studies have found that an organizational culture is not easily manipulated in intentional ways by managers (Ouchi and Wilkins, 1985: 476).

In his book *The Irrational Organization* Nils Brunsson analyses the need for organizational ideologies in order to enhance action within the organization. Ideologies, he says, 'focus the perceptions of its members on a few selected aspects of reality' (1985: 31). This makes people more confident. Ideologies are present in all organizations, because the main problem of an organization 'is not choosing; it is taking organized action' (1985: 31).

Alvesson (1990: 387, 391) discusses 'image orders' in organizations to compensate for increasing complexity and ambiguity in organizational life. An image order that includes activities that are loosely coupled to productivity and efficiency is created. He talks about pseudo-events, pseudo-actions and pseudo-structures.

The emphasis on organizational culture and image can be understood as forms of persuasion in Barnard's terminology. Scott (1992: 64) calls this a 'neo-Barnardian' perspective. Persuasion is rarely used instead of individual incentives, but it can be understood as a complement to wages, prestige, work environment etc. Even though an organizational culture is not based on individual performance control, it nevertheless often implies a symbolic control in terms of obedience and presence at rituals or ceremonies as well as a hierarchy (cf. Hechter, 1987: 159, 162; Heydebrand, 1989: 347).

Incentives and persuasion are centripetal forces in any organization contributing to the upkeep of authority. To the extent that individual affiliates can use their influence power, however, they can escape the internal control and perhaps change the structure of incentives to their own advantage without ever challenging the organizational authority as a whole.

Neither incentives nor persuasion are always enough to make people do what they should. In all organizations it happens now and then that affiliates do less than they are expected to. Control is rarely perfect, and the effect of persuasion fades after a time and has to be repeated. To the extent that affiliates can use their influence power they can get advantages if they get tired or fed up. And almost all affiliates have some influence power, since they usually know more about their own tasks and the conditions for carrying them out than anyone else. Influence power is based on the dependence of the organization on the tasks someone is supposed to fulfil, but the power of influence decreases with the increasing substitutability of the person occupying a particular position (see Hickson et al., 1971: 220–1).

The so-called 'agency theory' deals with problems that arise when one party delegates work to an agent, who performs that work. Agency theory is aimed at resolving conflicts about diverging goals in such relations and about the costs of monitoring the actions of the agent (see Eisenhardt, 1989: 58). Originally this theory was focused on relations between owners and managers (CEOs) in large corporations, but the problem is in principle the same in all relations between affiliates.

In his book *Manufacturing Consent* Michael Burawoy has given a lively description of the relations of dependence between workers in a machine shop in the United States. Operators with strategic jobs and particular skills 'are in a strong bargaining position *vis-à-vis* the scheduling man' to get the best paid jobs. To be able to make out, however, the operators are also dependent on a crib attendant to get good tools, and on truck drivers to get stocks for the machines in time (Burawoy, 1979: 52–3; see also the discussion in Silverman, 1971: 197–204).

Michel Crozier describes the power of maintenance workers in a French state owned tobacco plant. Since machine stoppages are frequent and disrupt the work process considerably, production workers are very dependent on the maintenance workers to fix stoppages, and supervisors do not have the skill to check on their work. This brings a great deal of autonomy to maintenance workers (Crozier, 1964: 108–9). Other similar relations of 'parallel power' are elements of what Crozier calls a 'bureaucratic vicious circle' (1964: 187, 192). Such a vicious circle is characterized by a disruption in the relations between positions in an organization that hinders the spread of information and orders. Much of this disruption is due to influence power of various origins.

Influence power is not only relevant in discussing individual affiliates. Groups of affiliates who have similar positions and similar interests may use their common influence power for their own (just or unjust) purposes in putting demands on a larger share of organizational resources or in changing relations between positions. Coalitions may be shifting due to changing purposes and interests. What goes on inside organizations is to a substantial extent determined by processes of bargaining between coalitions; thus 'conflict is never fully resolved within an organization' (Cyert and March, 1963: 43; cf. Clegg, 1989: 198). Coalitions may be formed by professional groups demanding autonomy or by workers demanding more power and influence in a corporation. In this way both contents of positions and relations among them can be changed through the internal struggle and bargaining going on.

# 6

# BETWEEN ORGANIZATIONS

## with Roine Johansson

### Social processes as organizational interaction

People encounter society through their organizational affiliations, and the positions they have in organizations. Within
each organization positions are coordinated, but organizations as social units are not coordinated into a higher order
such as a system or a society. In the social landscape there are
social phenomena other than organizations, for instance,
institutions, norms and languages, but there is no unit
having power or authority to command or structure organizations.

Macro-processes occur when organizations move or
expand in interaction with each other. Universal processes
such as the development of capitalism, industrialization,
democratization, the growth of world trade, the development of the welfare state, happen within and between
organizations, and not above them in the clouds of a system
or structure. Democratization or the growth of world trade
are social processes that are brought about by acting people.
Their actions are filtered in organizational positions and
accumulated through organizational coordination. Thus,
individual actions are multiplied into social processes.

Since organizations do not form societies or systems there are no capitalist, socialist or any other kinds of society. There are only constellations of organizations comprising several types of organization. In order to secure the supply of labour, enterprises have to interact with all types of organization, families, states as well as voluntary associations. There may be few or many capitalist enterprises within a particular part of the social landscape, but nowhere are there only capitalist enterprises. The influence of capitalist enterprises in a constellation of organizations is contingent upon their particular resources of power in relation to the resources of other organizations.

There are no democratic societies either. Democracy has to be understood in terms of relations between and within organizations. Shifts from democracy to dictatorship or vice versa are not changes in systems, but changes in relations between the state, parties and media organizations depending on the particular constellation of organizations in a country. It has been found that the existence of democracy in the countries of South America has been contingent upon the presence of strong conservative parties (see Rueschemeyer, et al., 1992: 287).

The 'Swedish model' for negotiations between employers and unions, and the welfare state, did not constitute a system. The breakdown of this model is a change in relations between enterprises, unions and the Swedish state. Even if this model has ceased to exist all the organizations that were part of it are still there. What has changed is their relative strength and, concomitantly, their interaction.

In social sciences there is confusion about what is going on between organizations. It is rarely analysed in terms of organizations at all, and often separated from its organizational context and seen as a system of interaction, for instance, corporatism, or as a distinct institution such as a market. But markets need to be analysed as 'relations among organizations' (Simon, 1991: 28; cf. Swedberg, 1993). In their research on banks in the United States Neil Fligstein and Peter Brantley (1992: 304) have found that a sociology of markets has to focus on 'inter- and intraorganizational politics'.

Most of the people in a market are affiliated with organizations and they often act on their behalf. Their resources come from organizations. Consumers to a large extent act on behalf of their families. Markets consist of semi-organized fields. Producers do not first of all watch what is on the market, they watch what other firms are doing (White, 1981: 518). What is called a market is a form of interaction between organizations, which often does not fit well with a notion of markets as a competition between a large number of actors who cannot by themselves affect what is going on.

Interaction between organizations is confusing to social scientists, since it necessarily crosses the boundaries of social science disciplines (see Ahrne, 1990: 99–103; Wallerstein, 1991: 271). Interactions between different types of organization have not been theorized adequately, partly because such interactions do not fit into any of the favoured discourses in disciplines such as economics or political science.

Most organizations are involved in both economic and political processes, and it is almost impossible to separate the one from the other. Business enterprises often have close connections with political parties and states, and many voluntary associations are involved in economic activities. In interaction between organizations economics and politics are not two distinct modes of interaction. We will argue that in order to analyse interaction between organizations, we first have to understand what constitutes the organizational capacity to act, which implies a discussion of power and resources. And resources such as money or weapons can be used for many purposes.

## Tools of power: relations and resources of power

The concept of power has a negative connotation. Those who talk about power have often been exposed to the negative aspects of power, for instance an environmental organization that has not been able to stop the construction of a new motorway, a person who has been dismissed from a job. In such situations the effects of power are experienced negatively.

For parties and government authorities that have been able to carry through their plans for a new road, or for the company that has rationalized its production, the effects of the same processes are part of their success. They probably do not talk about power at all.

Power is about being able to enforce intentions or interests, despite the fact that they 'affect B in a manner contrary to B's interests' (see Lukes, 1974: 27). It is a question of making B perform actions that B would not have done if it had not been for the actions or the intentions of A, or stopping B from doing something.

Power implies a capacity to act. In order to make another organization change its actions, or to stop it, you need to be able to act. Stopping something is an action in itself. 'In the broadest terms power has to do with getting things done, or with getting others to do them' (Barbalet, 1985: 538; cf. Giddens, 1984: 175). Mintzberg (1983: 4–5) points out that the French word *pouvoir* means both 'power' and 'to be able'.

Power is relational. If the relation between two or more organizations is based on direct dependence we can talk about power. Ties of mutual dependence imply that a party in a relation is 'in a position to grant or deny, facilitate or hinder, the other's gratification' (Emerson, 1962: 32). When an organization uses the dependence on its resources of another organization to make that organization do things it would not otherwise do, power is clearly involved. If a big company forces one of its subcontractors not to sell products to another company this act is a result of their relations of power.

The power of one organization has to be analysed in a context, in its relation to another organization and according to the particular dependence between them. A relation involving power is often obvious, but it may also be hidden, and power may be involved in relations to a greater or lesser extent. Resources of power may be useful without being used, and power does not necessarily have to be executed in order to be effective. Power is used strategically (Korpi, 1985).

We have suggested that human interaction can best be understood in terms of organizations. Thus, we will argue that the use of power in society needs to be analysed in connection with organizations, which are the primal 'power containers' (Giddens, 1984: 262; cf. Clegg, 1989: 17, 239). First of all, we need to differentiate between mechanisms of power inside and outside organizations. Inside organizations power rests on authority, and people's resistance can be analysed in terms of influence. We discussed this in chapter 5. Relations of power are tighter and more regulated inside than outside organizations. Compare the relations of a shopkeeper to his or her employees with relations to customers. Outside organizations power has to be understood in relations between organizations, that is, in encounters between power resources from different organizations. Relations of power outside organizations are more unpredictable than inside. Organizations do not obey each other, and there are no zones of indifference in relations between organizations (cf. Stinchcombe, 1990: 200–1).

There is no authority between organizations, no hierarchy and no subordination. Other organizations within the territory of a state are not affiliated with the state; they do not belong to the state. Only individuals are citizens. However, organizations can themselves join organizations, such as employers' organizations, the World Council of Churches, the International Olympic Committee. We will discuss such 'organizations of organizations' in chapter 7.

In interaction between organizations the power of any organization, however great, is limited by the power one or several other organizations have at their disposal (Etzioni, 1968: 314; Clegg, 1989: 208). Other organizations mobilize their own resources to resist or to defend themselves (Barbalet, 1985: 541).

When different types of organization confront each other in a struggle, different kinds of power resources may be in use, as in a struggle between a state and a corporation, or between unions and corporations. When different kinds of power collide the outcome may be hard to predict and assess. It is often difficult to see who is winning and who is losing (Ahrne, 1990: 101–2).

Resources are often material, for instance, buildings, machinery, and other kinds of property. Knowledge may be a resource, and all affiliates of an organization are resources in themselves through their commitment to do certain things. Most organizational resources are not primarily created to gain power over other organizations. However, as soon as some of the resources of an organization become the object of dependence of another organization, there is at least potentially a relation of power involved. Thus, most organizational resources can become involved in relations of power. As soon as one organization needs something from another organization, and alternatives are few, there is a potential relation of power. Almost all sorts of resources may be turned into tools of power.

Dependence can also be forced upon an organization through a threat. To utter threats usually accompanied by a demand is a method of establishing a relation of dependence involving resources of power. Laws of a state can be understood as generalized threats about measures that will be taken if an organization violates a law.

Many organizations, however, acquire and maintain resources primarily in order to become powerful and to be able to affect actions of other organizations. This is particularly the case for states and many voluntary associations. Such tools of power are inherently relational. Military weapons, for instance, are designed to create certain types of dependence. No tools of power are effective in all situations. Yet, some resources are more significant than others if they apply to a more varied scope of relations (Korpi, 1985: 34). Korpi mentions qualities of resources such as centrality and concentration to refer to different forms of applicability. The possession of money is probably the most general power resource 'with a large domain, high concentration potential as well as high convertibility, liquidity, scarcity, and storage potential' (Korpi, 1985: 34). But money cannot do everything. Money alone cannot buy commitment, at least not in the long run. The value of a particular set of resources is connected with the relation of dependence. Resources may become obsolete, like the Polish cavalry at the beginning of the Second World War, when they were confronted with German tanks. The potential power of a strike varies with how much employers depend on their employees at a certain time.

There are costs involved in using power resources (see Korpi, 1985: 33; cf. Etzioni, 1968: 316). One aim of possessing power is to be able to make another organization do things it would not otherwise do. If it can be achieved without having to waste resources so much the better. In many cases people in the other organization will perform these actions because they anticipate what will happen if they do not. Mere threats to use power are often enough to get things done. Whether demands are met or not is to a large extent due to their credibility. Thus, the power of one organization rests upon what affiliates of the other organization believe is going to happen if they do not live up to the demands of the more powerful organization.

Most relations of power probably take place without any power resources being used. Making threats credible without having to go into full action is the most rational way of using power. The full use of the power resources of two organizations in an open conflict is unusual. This is a reason why many relations of power are not easily visible.

When interaction between organizations is adjusted to their relations of power it usually only rests on how the interacting parties perceive the resources of power involved in the interaction. Their estimations may be wrong, but it is impossible to know without really using resources in a conflict. Etzioni discusses the poor knowledge that organizational representatives have of their power, and he argues that this fact explains the occurrence of conflicts. However, the opposite may also be true. If perceptions of power are wrong, there may be many organizations that have under-estimated their own power to resist and thus have conceded too easily. On the other hand, it is probably true, as Etzioni argues, that the number of conflicts would be greatly reduced if 'the relative power of various societal units were comple-tely measurable' (Etzioni, 1968: 319). If power resources were completely known beforehand the outcome of a conflict would also be known, and people who know that they will lose are not likely to go into an open conflict.

## Competition, conflict, collaboration and exchange

In much social theory organizations are either treated as independent of each other, or as belonging to a system. In real social life, however, organizations are heavily involved in interaction with many other organizations. For their activities organizations depend on other organizations, but not on all others. Some organizations are more significant than others. An organization may be involved in different forms of interaction with different significant other organiz-ations. But for any organization at a certain time most organizations are only indirectly related to its activities.

Interaction between organizations is instrumental and strategic. In order to achieve goals and to gain resources, organizations can either cooperate with other organizations, or they can struggle against them. But struggle between organizations does not preclude cooperation; 'every re-lationship between firms is, in our view, both competitive and cooperative' (Axelsson, 1992: 200). Analytically, how-ever, we will discuss struggle and cooperation as two distinct forms of interaction.

Patterns of interaction can be related to whether resources that interacting organizations try to get hold of are the

**Position of resources**

| | | Inside | Outside |
|---|---|---|---|
| | Struggle | Conflict | Competition |
| **Form of interaction** | | | |
| | Cooperation | Exchange | Collaboration |

Figure 1   *Forms of interaction between organizations*

property of or in the control of any one of them, or if the resources are situated outside their relationship. We will distinguish between four patterns of interaction between organizations. A conflict between organizations is a struggle for resources that one or both of them have within their control. A competition is a struggle for resources that are outside their control. Cooperation may happen either as a collaboration to get hold of resources owned or controlled by neither of them, or as an exchange of resources between them (see figure 1).

In an open conflict the dependency between the organizations involved is great, and they have few alternatives. Wars and strikes are examples of conflicts where organizations are struggling for resources, for instance, land or money, that the other organization controls. In conflicts organizations try to hurt each other in order to obtain resources from the other organizations or to defend their own resources. In open conflicts tools and resources of power are used to gain other resources. Often open conflicts happen because people in the organizations involved are uncertain about their own strength.

Competition is another pattern of struggle between organizations. As Georg Simmel has pointed out, in competition the conflict between parties is indirect. 'The aim for which competition occurs within a society is presumably always the favor of one or more third persons' (Simmel, 1964: 61).

Parties compete for the support of voters, and corporations compete for customers.

That competition is indirect implies that it is a more elusive form of struggle than a conflict. It is not always clear when a competition begins or ends or who the competitors are. Competition can involve organizations from several sectors, which makes the competition more confused. In some competitons, however, relations are more direct, and all competitors known. Such is the case in a political election or in sports. Sometimes competitors may be directly confronted with each other, as in a debate before an election or in soccer games. There are no constructed arenas for open conflicts, only for competitions, for instance, marketplaces, stadiums, parliament buildings and exhibition halls.

Since interaction in competitions is indirect, an analysis of power is not as relevant for competitions as for conflicts. Competitors are not supposed to use power resources against each other, only their strength. They are generally not supposed to obstruct others, but to perform better than the others. In competitions involving a direct confrontation there may be more opportunities to use resources of power. And, of course, many organizations use tools of power against competitors, even though they are not supposed to.

When cooperation between two (or more) organizations involves resources that one or both of the organizations control, we usually talk about a relationship of exchange. Since exchange implies a dependence between two organizations it often involves the use of power resources (Korpi, 1985: 35). Conflicts are often resolved by an agreement on a form of exchange, for instance, a peace treaty about the transfer of territory from one state to another or an agreement between employers and a union about wages. Most forms of exchange, though, are not preceded by open conflict. A relationship of exchange may be occasional, such as in the case of the purchase of a commodity, or it may be long-lasting, for instance, the renting or leasing of property. Exchange relationships between organizations may be stabilized, 'if the heterogenous resources controlled by the actors become adapted to each other and become highly special-ized' (Mattsson and Johansson, 1992: 208). Axelsson (1992: 198) maintains that most cooperation between corporations 'lie[s] in everyday informal activities within continuing business relationships'. Yet, there are clearly a substantial number of formal contractual relations between organiz-ations to regulate the exchange between them.

Oliver Williamson (1991) discusses 'hybrid forms of organ-izations' such as networks or joint ventures. In his later writings he has acknowledged that there are alternative solutions between hierarchical organization and pure market exchange to reduce transaction costs. In some instances the problem of transaction costs can be approached through contracts. Stinchcombe (1990: 233) suggests that greater uncertainty regarding client specifications, costs and perfor-mance measures makes for organizational solutions. In other cases agreements and contracts between firms are better ways to secure a continuity, and still maintain a flexibility.

Other patterns of cooperation are cartels and alliances. Here organizations collaborate in order to achieve common goals that are outside their control. The goal of such collaboration is often to create a 'negotiated environment' (Pfeffer and Salancik, 1978) that serves the interest of all organizations involved. Instead of competing organizations may collaborate in secret, in order to control prices or political alternatives. Organizations may also collaborate to fight against common enemies. Social movements are gener-ally made up of organizations collaborating for a common cause.

Cooperation does not preclude struggle. The interaction between parties in a coalition government is often character-ized by as much struggle as cooperation. Interaction between teams in a soccer league is more cooperation than compe-tition. They cooperate in making schedules for the games, in sharing the income from spectators, in recruiting referees, etc. The moment of competition in their interaction is marginal.

Most interaction between organizations is contingent on

their relations of power, although nobody knows exactly which these relations are. A conflict presupposes that affiliates of at least one of the organizations involved want to test their power, and believe that they have something to gain.

Conditions for the stabilization of relations of power between organizations are determined through negotiations. A negotiation is a transitory form of interaction, where relations of power are discussed and often confirmed in agreements. Instead of wasting their resources in conflicts or competition organizations start to talk about them. Negotiations also take place when a relation of interaction is to be continued. Contractual relations between firms are often renegotiated. Negotiations between employers and unions mirror new estimations of their relations of power. Finally, negotiations also take place at the beginning of a cooperation between organizations that did not interact with each other before.

A negotiation is an arrangement between organizations to evaluate their respective power resources. They may have resources of different kinds, but each party has to compare and estimate their own resources in relation to the other party's resources. There is no obvious method for comparing divergent resources of power, but such a comparison has to be made if an agreement is to be reached. Negotiation is a way for organizations to make agreements on the exchange rate of their respective resources of power.

## Negotiations: talking about power

Power resources may be effective without being used. In negotiations between organizations power is important, but the idea of a negotiation is that the parties involved will not use their power resources, only talk about them. But it is difficult to talk about power, and initially negotiators often try to support their demands through arguments about fairness and objectivity. In investigating negotiations it can be demonstrated how people in organizations handle resources of power and how they are perceived.

A negotiation between two organizations is a way to stabilize their interaction. In the interaction following a negotiation relations of power are often hidden and forgotten. But analysing the negotiations unveils the underlying relations of power in such an interaction.

A negotiation is a phase of transition between modes of interaction. A negotiation is opened when actors from two organizations come to realize that they have some mutual interests in changing their relations and stabilizing their interaction. The greatest problem in starting a negotiation may be to get to know whether the other organization is interested in a change, too, because asking for negotiations may often be controversial. Even if it is not possible to say exactly when negotiations start, it is usually easy to know when they have stopped either through an agreement or through a withdrawal of one or both of the parties from the interaction, possibly followed by an open conflict.

There are always limits to the mutual interests in a negotiation. Such interests can be seen as being within a contract zone. Demands and offers from the parties that are outside the contract zone will not lead to an agreement, 'because one or the other party would be better off without an agreement' (Bacharach and Lawler, 1981: 5). A problem, though, is that one of the uncertainties in negotiations is for each party to know the limits of the other party. Moreover, limits may change over time. If a process of negotiation goes on for some time, 'an agreement may finally be reached, but in the meantime much of the gain from cooperation has been squandered' (Elster, 1989: 70).

Negotiations take place between a small and limited number of organizations in direct interaction and communication in a situation characterized by uncertainty. During the process of negotiation each of the parties involved may try to enhance their positions through strategical manoeuvres. Since negotiations are processes of interaction that take time and are situated within a wider social context, where information is incomplete, game theory is unable to explain the outcome of negotiations between organizations (see Bacharach and Lawler, 1981: 16–17; Elster, 1989: 82–6).

Ongoing negotiations between two organizations do not preclude other forms of interaction between them. Phases of interaction may overlap. Negotiations may be opened while an open conflict or competition is still going on. Negotiations may be secret, or they may not cover all aspects of the interaction between the parties involved.

There are several reasons for keeping the initial phase of negotiations secret. If there are disagreements within one or both of the organizations, initial contacts could be unfeasible if they were known and be obstructed by opponents from within. Starting negotiations may also lower the morale of affiliates, for instance, in a war or a competition between business rivals. Negotiations between two political parties may be controversial both for representatives of other parties and for sympathizers. Negotiations and possible agreements between two corporations may be kept totally secret if they violate laws, or general notions of a fair competition.

Although negotiations necessarily imply direct contacts between the organizations involved, it seems that much of what determines the outcome does not happen in the direct confrontation between parties. How organizations prepare for negotiations is of great significance for the results. Preparations are aimed at increasing the strength of the organization in relation to the other organization. One way to achieve this is to search for alternatives to decrease the dependence. Another way is to mobilize resources within the organization or possibly to find support from other parties to increase the dependence of the other organization.

To have alternative solutions or options for new forms of interaction raises the threshold for what an organization will accept. Alternatives can be looked for before or during ongoing negotiations (Bacharach and Lawler, 1981: 63; Ury, 1993: 22–3). It is a matter of strategy in an actual contact with the other party if, when and how such alternatives will be used as arguments. In an ongoing negotiation between two political parties an open search for alternatives may only be obstructive, whereas existence of alternatives is less controversial in relations between business enterprises. Many business negotiations, in fact, start with a search process. The possibility of finding alternatives is connected with the degree of flexibility and mobility of organizations.

The other way of increasing the relative power in preparations for negotiations is to mobilize resources and affiliates of the organization, which requires coordination. One important aspect is the formulation of demands and the necessity for creating unity around them. How demands are formulated is a result of the type of organization. To agree on demands is more complicated in states and voluntary associations than in corporations. Yet, it seems that it is important in all types of organization to have a clear notion of the acceptable outcome in order to negotiate successfully. For the people actually having the contacts with representatives of the other organizations, it helps to have a clear mandate for what can be accepted or not. The representatives of the other party need to know to what extent they can trust what a negotiator offers. One solution when a negotiation has come to a standstill may be to engage top leaders with undisputed competence to make final bids and concessions (March, 1988: 50). But there also need to be arrangements for how negotiators can communicate with the rest of the organization and ask for support if the negotiations take an unexpected turn. Other affiliates need to have faith in what the negotiators do and the results they have achieved. For trade union negotiators it may sometimes be useful to portray negotiations as tougher than they really are in order to get support from their members. But unions can also increase their resources in negotiations if they can demonstrate that their members are prepared to fight for their demands (Heckscher, 1993: 91–2).

If negotiations have started in secret it may be an even bigger problem to get support from the rest of the organization. A proposal of a merger between the two big car manufacturers in Sweden, Volvo and Saab, that had been negotiated in secret between the top executive of Volvo and the main owner of Saab was turned down by the board of the Saab corporation (see Gyllenhammar, 1991: 28–36).

Another way of mobilizing power is to try to find allies to join the negotiations or at least to get support from other organizations or from the general public. Unions may try to create cartels with other unions to negotiate with the same employer, and corporations may join together in order to get better terms in negotiations to buy larger quantities.

When demands have been formulated, it seems that much of the time during contacts between negotiators is spent discussing technical matters relating to possible future interaction. A third element of the direct negotiations is the talk about power. Here we can distinguish three ways to introduce power into the talks: threats, warnings and bluffs. Threats are about what the organization will do if demands are not accepted (see Bacharach and Lawler, 1981: 133–4). Threats may be followed up by a demonstration of readiness to use power. William Ury mentions a strategy among Japanese workers to 'wear black armbands in order to let management know the depth of their grievances' (1993: 138). A threat, however, may be perceived as a confrontation, whereas a warning may appear more objective and respectful even if the content is the same (Ury, 1993: 137; cf. Elster, 1992: 122–4). A warning implies that the negotiator cannot take on the responsibility for how other affiliates, members or managers, will react. A threat indicates what the members of an organization will do if their demands are not met, while a warning is about what will happen.

Bluffs are possible in negotiations since power resources are not used, only talked about. A bluff is 'an attempt to exaggerate one's own power' (Bacharach and Lawler, 1981: 171). Bluffs may be constructed on statements of the militancy of members, the amount of resources, the interest and dependence on the outcome of the negotiations, or various other matters. But bluffing is risky. If bluffs are not credible they may have an opposite effect, and especially in negotiations that will lead to long-term relations bluffs may threaten the future interaction.

Like all activities of organizations negotiations rely on acting individuals. A situation where organizations mobilize resources in confrontation with another organization is characterized by an unusual uncertainty. Because of the greater uncertainty the matter of how to handle individuals acting on behalf of organizations gets increased attention. Decisions taken during negotiations are not routine decisions, and it is more important than usual for an organization to show a united facade (see March, 1988: 68–9). Unity gives strength, and adversaries or enemies will try to use any signs of disagreement between affiliates to their own advantange. This is also the case in open conflicts, for instance, wars or strikes. But since organizations are not monolithic units, they will have to find ways to establish unity or to hide and control disagreements.

But the other organization may try to appeal to a negotiator as part human to make him or her softer, and to destroy the unity. Offering personal advantages or gains to a negotiator may be one way of getting a better agreement for the other party. It seems that too friendly a contact between two negotiators may raise suspicions among other affiliates of either organization that their negotiator has given in too easily. When the Swedish employers' organization, SAF, changed their strategy towards a more militant ideological approach to wage negotiations, they replaced many negotiators who were considered to be too lenient and too much involved with trade union representatives.

A team of negotiators are more vulnerable if they are isolated from their own organization. The strategy of a transnational corporation in the United States was to invite clients out on their yacht to 'gain the advantage of removing them from phones, interruptions, and distractions while severely limiting their access to information' (Adler, 1991: 189). Another way to use the personal situation of negotiators, particularly if they are away from their organization and their family, is to stretch their time constraints. A corporation in Brazil were able to get a favourable agreement in this way. The negotiators from the United States wanted to go home for Christmas and were willing as time passed to make substantial concessions to be able to do so (Adler, 1991: 191; cf. Hintze, 1988: 65).

On the other hand, personal acquaintances and networks may be useful, particularly in the initial phases of negotiations, or in order to establish contacts between two organizations. It has been reported from the peace negotiations between Israel and the Palestinians that old relations of friendship were decisive in renewing talks between the parties. An Israeli historian, who had been working with economic development in the territories occupied by Israel, and who had good relations with the PLO, also happened to be a childhood friend of the vice Foreign Secretary of Israel. Through his mediation new contacts between the parties could be established.

Negotiation is a way for organizations to make agreements by comparing their power resources. This is by no means an easy task, but comparisons have to be made if an agreement is to be reached. Organizations try to increase the predictability of the process by applying different methods of coordination and resource mobilization. Such methods can, however, only decrease and never eliminate the element of uncertainty. Negotiations are inherently unpredictable.

# 7

# IN THE THICK OF
# ORGANIZATIONS

## with Apostolis Papakostas

### Local activities, global interaction

People depend on organizations for survival as well as for pleasure. Most everyday life activities take place in the realms of organizations, either inside them or in semi-organized fields. People move between organizations on a daily basis, going to their job, going home, going shopping, going to church etc. Everyday life is situated in the world within one's reach (Schutz, 1962: 224). Thus, people who live in the same area (village, town, valley etc.) form a community.

The constellation of organizations, however, that supply the positions for everyday life activities do not form communities. Cooperation as well as struggle between organizations happen on a global scale; they are worldwide and transcend any boundaries of communities or societies. Business enterprises may have branches in several communities and countries. Even a single small enterprise in a town may depend more for its production, or for selling its products, on organizations situated in far away places. The local congregation may be part of a worldwide church.

Spatial proximity among organizations does not coincide with relations of interdependence. Thus, to explain and understand changes in everyday activities in organizational positions, we have to consider dependencies and interaction between organizations that stretch beyond a local or regional community, that is to say, that which is often considered a society. Human actions and activities are locally situated, but their preconditions and causes are global.

In a particular place in the social landscape there is a constellation of organizations, but the organizations may not have more in common than that they happen to be geographically close: a nuclear power plant close to a couple of farms, a small town with a church, a gas station and a soccer field, a tourist hotel in a fishing village. Neither the origin nor the interdependencies of the organizations in these constellations can be comprehended by analysing a geographically distinct constellation. For the supply of affiliates organizations depend on local communities of people, but for the supply of other resources such as raw material, products and knowledge, organizations to a large extent depend on and interact with other organizations outside the obvious geographical constellation. On the local scene organizations turn up or disappear by the push and pull of invisible distant forces in other parts of the social landscape.

Unlike concepts such as 'populations' of organizations (see Aldrich, 1992: 19), or 'organizational fields' (see DiMaggio and Powell, 1991b: 64–5), which denote similarities between organizations, the concept of constellation emphasizes the geographical closeness between organizations. But this closeness does not necessarily imply a similarity. A constellation of organizations is not integrated: it is only a number of organizations that happen to exist in the same vicinity at the same time, but with different origin, and with different futures and relations of interdependence.

A constellation is no organized order, nor is it unordered or chaotic; it is a frozen disorder, where relations of dependence and power are hidden. Constellations are 'the tangible compromises made in specific places between workers and employers, developers and consumers, entrepreneurs and creative personnel' (Zukin, 1991: 22). A constellation of organizations is a description of the organizations that are relevant for a group of people in their everyday lives. Organizations within a constellation do not necessarily interact with each other, but cooperation or competition takes place with various other organizations as well. Still, organizational positions set the frames for everyday life.

If interdependencies of organizations in a constellation stretch out in several directions and into various distances, it is impossible to see a constellation as a system. In a system it should be possible to regard the parts as 'directly and indirectly related in a causal network' (Buckley, 1967: 41), and it should be possible to distinguish between exogenous and endogenous variables (Elster, 1983: 42). Thus, we do not think it is a useful solution to the problem of the fluidity of the concept of society to talk about 'intersocietal systems' (see Giddens, 1984: 184, 1990b: 303).

No constellation of organizations can be understood in isolation from the surrounding terrain. Any boundary of a constellation is arbitrary. Constellations change through the spread of new organizational forms and through the concomitant change or decline of already existing organizations. A constellation of organizations does not form a distinct regime or a culture, nor can it be treated as an isolated case. Instead of cases we can talk about instances; an instance being 'a place, within a far larger plane of occurrence, where the working of the processes are directly observable or clearly traceable through their effects' (Hopkins, 1982: 31). This does not necessarily imply that universal processes explain all local events. Causal explanations in the social sciences are usually 'combinations of conditions that produce change'. Change emerges 'from the appropriate intersection of appropriate preconditions' (Ragin, 1987: 25). Organizational forms have a history and explanation of their own, independent of the local constellation. This history must be part of a relevant 'causal story' (Davidson, 1980).

New organizational forms may spread as universal institutional processes, and there is an interplay between universalistic processes and particularistic constellations (Robertson, 1992: 99–103). New forms are spread through the diffusion of knowledge, technology, demands etc., and through active intervention and promotion by particular organizations in selling new products and establishing new plants, or through mission and agitation. The outcome of such processes is contingent on relations of power in each place. The point we want to make here is that the outcome of the same universal institutional process, for instance, democratization or the establishing of welfare states, is different in different constellations of organizations. Since universal processes encounter different local reception and resistance, globalization does not necessarily imply a homogenization. Global processes may just as well imply new forms of differentiation (cf. Arnason, 1990: 224).

Worldwide interaction between organizations is not a recent phenomenon. In all human history organizations and institutions have been spread and moved across the world, thereby establishing new forms of interdependence. The difference now is in the intensity of these interrelations through new forms of communication. Thereby the global processes have been more concentrated in time and thus more obvious. Roland Robertson (1992: 58–60) has analysed the 'temporal-historical path to the present circumstance of a very high degree of global density and complexity'.

Regime is another word for system. By using the analogy of regime, internal interaction is emphasized at the cost of a consideration of the encounter between universal processes and local circumstances. The establishment of welfare states is a universal institutional idea and process supported by political parties and unions, and resisted in various degrees by other organizations in all countries. The effect of this ongoing struggle varies between states and countries. The process is similar but the outcome is different in varying constellations due to relations of power. When Gøsta Esping-Andersen (1990) in his book *The Three Worlds of Welfare*

*Capitalism* clusters different states into 'three distinct regimes' – a liberal, a social democratic and a corporatist welfare state – he overemphasizes the similarity between some regimes and the differences between others. He also overemphasizes the stability of regimes (Kangas, 1991: 102). Boundaries between regimes are arbitrary, as has been demonstrated by Castles and Mitchell (1992), who argue for a distinction between four types of welfare state using somewhat different measures. We do not want to argue that any effort of classification is better than another, only to suggest that the debate about welfare state regimes demonstrates the problem of looking at constellations as totalities.

The problem of labelling and analysing constellations of organizations as regimes is well illustrated if one compares various such efforts that never seem to coincide. Jepperson and Meyer (1991: 216), for instance, offer a quite different categorization of 'rationalized polities' from Esping-Andersen, while Burawoy (1985: 138) offers yet another categorization of 'factory regimes'.

Another prevalent method of delimiting areas of the social landscape as distinct entities is to regard certain nations or communities as 'cultures'. A culture is supposed to present actors within its domain with certain common traits and patterns of acting and thinking that render a causal primacy to the cultural sphere in explaining organizational phenomena within a distinct society. Crozier (1964: 212, 251) outlined such an approach in his analysis of the vicious circle in the French bureaucracy. He argued that the same 'overtones' of culture were predominant also in the French labour movement, for instance. The cultural approach as an explanation of organizational forms has been most pronounced in analysing and explaining organizations in Japan.

A culturalist explanation of differences does not get much support, however, from the results of a large survey of organizational structures and employees of similar plants in seven industrial branches in Japan and the United States. Overall, the findings indicate striking similarities in the connections between organizational variables, positions, commitment and job satisfaction among Japanese and US employees. According to the researchers differences between the countries in terms of organizational structure should rather be explained as a consequence of the late development of Japanese industry and particular circumstances during the introduction of industrial manufacturing in Japan. For instance, the large prevalence of quality circle programmes among employees in Japan can be explained in these terms. Moreover, according to a culturalist explanation one would not expect similar effects from quality circles in Japan as in the United States. According to these surveys, however, quality circles in both countries 'significantly raised employee teamwork, social integration and commitment' (Lincoln and Kalleberg, 1990: 251).

In an analysis of differences in business structure and business networks in Japan, South Korea and Taiwan, Hamilton and Biggart (1992) discard a one-sided culturalist explanation to these differences. Despite the fact that these three countries share many cultural patterns the organizational structure of the industry is vastly different. Hamilton and Biggart (1992: 200–8) suggest an alternative explanation in terms of different relations between the state and the business sector in these countries. These differences can be attributed to relations between political parties and the state at the end of the Second World War and its aftermath in the region, but also to the relations between business and kinship.

Other studies have pointed to the differences between organizations within the same culture, a fact that would also speak against a culturalist explanation (see Heller et al., 1988: 223–4). Even the survival of an old organizational form such as small bakeries in France can be explained in terms of the relations between the French peasantry and urban bakeries, rather than in terms of French culture or preferences among French consumers (see Clegg, 1990: 108–16).

Our conclusion from these studies is that the interaction between organizations and thus constellations of organizations is more important to explain the emergence of forms and structure of organizations than is a cultural homogeneity within particular cultures or societies. There is a 'myth of cultural integration' (Archer, 1990: 116). However, this does not preclude all influences from cultural processes on what goes on inside and between organizations. In a survey comparing employees in several Indian and English companies it was found that the structure and control strategies were influenced by the overall organizational environment, but job descriptions and communication inside the organizations were explained by cultural factors (Tayeb, 1988: 150). In their study Lincoln and Kalleberg (1990: 251) found that the influence of culture was indirect, and Hamilton and Biggart (1992: 182) conclude that organizations 'often employ cultural understandings' in strategies of control. This is also consistent with Hofstede's (1991) discussion of dimensions of national cultures in terms of, for instance, power distance and uncertainty avoidance. Such differences may well explain differences in what is going on between people inside organizations, but they do not seem to explain differences in organizational forms and structure. Moreover, cultural norms probably affect the family as an organization more than the business enterprise.

## Time sequences and the founding of organizations

The emergence of a new form of organization such as a new industry, a new church or a new party is generally due to unique combinations of processes that happen to coincide in a particular constellation at a particular time. New organizational forms are often produced by chance (Aldrich, 1986: 69–71; Zolberg, 1986: 435). Their origin can be explained by a peculiar combination of processes within the constellation. Fundamental changes in large organizations are rare, and they are often results of sudden shocks from actions taken by other organizations (Fligstein, 1991: 317–18). The emergence of new organizational forms happens stepwise. It is not a gradual transformation of previous forms. New forms are created in waves followed by periods of stabilization with few changes (see Astley, 1985).

The success story of the computing industry in Silicon Valley was the effect of many unique conditions in this constellation of organizations comprising universities, state agencies, city administration and private business. The whole constellation of organizations in Silicon Valley cannot be moved or transferred anywhere else. There have been many failures in efforts to recreate the complete constellation (see Sahlin-Andersson, 1990: 85–7). Only single organizations can spread or move, and in other constellations their position will be different.

How can an organization be established in a constellation where it has not originated, where conditions for its creation apparently were not present? Either it may be brought there, or it forces itself into the constellation. We can also ask whether a new organizational form would ever have originated in a particular constellation if it had not been brought there. One way of analysing the spread of organizations is to say that it is premature, that it takes place before the appropriate conditions prevail within a constellation. Such an argument implies that there is a natural sequence of development of organizations within different constellations. The frequent occurrence of real organizational diffusion, however, contradicts the idea of natural sequences of development. But the time sequence of the introduction of organizational forms in constellations has an effect on the particular design of the organization, which is contingent on relations with other organizations to the extent that it depends on them for the supply of resources, as labour power or members.

Since there are processes of diffusion of several forms of organizations in many directions simultaneously the variations in time sequences are substantial. The design of one form of organization depends on the presence or absence of other organizations in the constellation, that is, whether it is established before or after a particular other form of organization (see Aldrich, 1990: 20; Fulcher, 1991: 4). In comparative research this phenomenon has been discussed as timing. It has often been found to be of decisive importance, but it has not gained appropriate attention as a distinct phenomenon in analysing processes of evolution or change. Different time sequences in the founding of new organizations are a way of explaining differences between unions, churches or plants in different constellations of organizations that does not involve cultural explanations. The effect of timing has to do with the encounter between historical alternatives and particular local constellations of organizations.

Clark Kerr and his collaborators (1960: 103–6) discussed the phenomenon of historical timing in their description of 'the industrialization process'. First of all they discussed consequences of an early versus a late industrialization of a country. They noticed different relations between enterprises and labour organizations in a later industrialization. For them this was a problem, since, as they argued, labour organizations 'may not be well suited to the problems of countries at early stages of industrialization' (Kerr et al., 1960: 104). In his book *British Factory – Japanese Factory*, Ronald Dore also recognized the importance of the timing of relations between the establishment of enterprises and labour unions. His conclusions, however, are different. 'Japanese employers, therefore, knew that they had to live with unions at an early stage; they were able to adjust to that future prospect by institutional innovations *before* the unions became so strong that their options were foreclosed while they still had a large measure of control over the situation' (Dore, 1973: 410).

Michael Burawoy agrees with Dore's arguments, and he finds similarities in the form of unions in Japan and the United States. In both countries unions are prevalent in the monopoly sector of industry. Burawoy (1985: 66–7) argues that this phenomenon 'can be attributed to the absence of a strong industrial unionism prior to the emergence of large corporations'. Differences between union organizations in different countries in terms of their organizing principles, whether they recruit members according to craft or to industry, can also be attributed to the historical timing of the establishment of capitalist manufacturing and the founding of unions (see Therborn, 1983: 53). Burawoy adds that the early existence of political rights in the United States also contributed to weaker incentives for the establishment of labour organizations. This is also a conclusion of Lipset's (1983) discussion of the sources of working-class politics. The absence of a working-class party in the United States is partly due to the early enfranchisement of the white working class (Lipset, 1983: 6). The early establishment of two strong parties made it harder for new parties to emerge and gain a foothold.

The structure of political parties is contingent on whether they were established before or after trade unions became strong. According to Stinchcombe (1965: 164) this fact can account for differences between the Democratic Party in the United States and the Labour Party in Britain. Even more processes and thus more complicated sequences can be brought into the analysis. To explain the strong labour organizations in Sweden and the close relations between unions and the social-democratic party, it is interesting to recognize that the late establishment of unions in Sweden, which was due to late industrialization, made up for a coincidence of union organization and the advent of a socialist ideology. Union organizing was partly led by the new social-democratic party and inspired by socialist ideas. James Fulcher compares Britain and Sweden, and he concludes, 'socialism was available as the Swedish working class was formed and the Social Democratic Party did not face bourgeois parties already anchored in the working class' (as in Britain) (Fulcher, 1991: 70).

If an organization is established in a constellation of other organizations, its design has to be adjusted to available resources. Which these resources are is to a large extent governed by what resources are tied up by other organiz-ations, and what resources are directly available for a new organization. Stinchcombe (1965: 164, 167) has pointed out that organizational forms developed at different times are systematically different. They are much like houses built at different times. Stinchcombe explained this in terms of access to resources, above all wealth and the supply of labour. The positions and the structure of a new industry have to be designed according to the available supply of labour power in a certain constellation. And the supply of labour depends partly on what other industries there are, but also on whether trade unions are established within the constellation or not. As Landes (1986) pointed out, in England it was often easier to establish new industries in the countryside, where there was a different supply of labour power than in cities.

Sometimes new organizations establish themselves through coercion and the use of violence. They acquire resources by force through conquests. Generally, however, new organizations have to find free resources to use, or make new resources available, for instance, the recruitment of women from unpaid activities in the home to wage labour. They have to find 'open environmental space' or 'niches' to establish themselves (Astley, 1985: 233–4). And qualities of such open spaces tend to shape the particular organizational design. The first type of organization that arrives in an open space will occupy the resources and obstruct further exploitation.

New organizations have to be much more able to free resources that are already occupied. They have to pay higher wages, for instance, or offer better job opportunities. For people it is a larger step to change organizational affiliation, for instance employment, than to try shopping in another store. The risk involved in changing affiliation is greater. Loyalty, routine and invested resources tie people to their old affiliations.

Once an organization is established within a constellation, its centripetal forces tend to keep its structure and hierarchy intact. Organizations tend to be inert (see Hannan and Freeman, 1989: 33; Aldrich, 1992: 19). The structure of an organization is designed according to its original activities. All organizations are not equally inert though. Of the four types of organization we have distinguished, capitalist enterprises are more likely to change than other types, although all enterprises are not equally flexible or movable. A mining company is more tied to a certain area and a certain constellation of other organizations than a construction company.

States are less flexible; they cannot move and they cannot choose their citizens. Yet, states do change their form. States, however, are multidimensional and ambiguous; they have annual rings (see Ahrne, 1990: 108–9). States adjust to changing circumstances at the same time as they keep old imprints from earlier periods. As an organizational form the family has been remarkably tenacious, because of its ability to adjust to changing circumstances.

Voluntary associations are also relatively inert. They depend on members in a certain geographical region. The members of a voluntary association in general have a great loyalty to their organization, and they have invested a lot of resources into it. Stein Rokkan (1967: 191) has noted an 'organizational lag' when it comes to political parties. For most people in Western Europe 'the currently active parties have been part of the political landscape since their child-hood' (Lipset and Rokkan, 1967: 50). The opposite is true of Eastern Europe, where the breakdown of earlier state authorities created large open spaces for the establishment of many new parties in a short time.

## Growth, spread and interdependence of organizations

It seems to be an inherent force in most organizing endeavours to grow and expand. As a consequence they spread into new terrain, into new constellations of organiz-ations in the social landscape. Most of the organizations within a constellation were once newcomers. Organizations grow and spread both within and between countries, wherever they can find fertile land and new niches. The spread is not automatic: it often fails and it encounters resistance and competition. The incentive for most affiliates to make the organization bigger is in general a combination of the wish to acquire larger resources for all affiliates to enjoy, and an urge to spread a message and to change the world.

For most capitalist enterprises growth is a prerequisite for survival. To be competitive in the long run, business enterprises need to increase their resources and to find new customers. They also need to increase productivity by more efficient technology, or by trying to recruit employees willing to work for lower wages (see Wallerstein, 1990: 36–7; Dicken, 1992: 145–6).

The mission to spread the gospel is most obvious in churches of various types. The spread of the organization was formulated as one of the most important duties of a believer right at the start of Christianity. But this desire is equally strong in many other voluntary associations such as parties, unions, temperance organizations, peace organizations etc.

It is often impossible to distinguish between the motives to acquire resources and to spread a message. They are intertwined. For many voluntary associations it is essential to increase their resources and thereby their power. And enterprises, too, may have messages. The owner and founder of the Swedish transnational furniture producer and seller IKEA once wrote that it was the duty of IKEA to expand and contribute to a process of democratization.

In the course of the spread of organizations types of human activity may change form. Education may be changed from the family to the state, games among friends and neighbours may be transformed into organized competition and exercise in sports clubs.

Since most organizations are fixed by the time of their establishment in a particular constellation, we need to consider their origins and trace their historical roots in order to explain their present characteristics. We will distinguish between three ways in which organizations come to penetrate new terrain and occupy new parts of the social landscape. These three ways imply different causal relations. We will discuss organizational growth and enlargement, institutional processes and isomorphism and, finally, the movement of organizations.

## Growth and enlargement

The common way for business enterprises to grow is to build new production units and to open shops and offices attracting new employees and new customers. Growth necessarily implies expansion and spread into new geographical areas. And this is a form of diffusion, even if it happens within one and the same organization. More and more the growth of enterprises is spread into other countries. The investments and subsidiaries of large transnational corporations have multiplied at least ten times since the end of the Second World War (Dicken, 1992: 51–3).

The establishment of new shops is accompanied by the enlargement of semi-organized fields and often involves various forms of promotion. Thus, the new terrain is prepared. Yet, success is not automatic, and new establishments often fail. The spread of an enterprise into new terrain, new 'markets', may often be facilitated through networks of relations. To have a position in a network gives a better orientation in the new terrain and facilitates the timing of the founding of a new establishment (see Axelsson and Johansson, 1992: 231–4).

Enterprises also grow through mergers or simply through the purchase of other enterprises. These methods of enlargement cannot be considered a spread, but they still create new forms of interdependencies within constellations and among affiliates, even without their choice or knowledge.

There is often a resistance and hostility towards strangers. Often, when a transnational enterprise buys a local company they do not change the name of that company, in order not to create unnecessary hostility. Likewise, many transnational companies sell their products under many labels to conceal the true relations of dependence. This strategy is common in the food and beverage industry, for instance. Keeping the name of local producers gives the product a local flavour, although it is produced by a transnational enterprise.

On the other hand, enterprises that grow and spread though the establishment of the same concept in new places such as McDonald's or IKEA try to profit from their common transnational image. Yet, their image cannot be the same as in their place of origin. IKEA, for instance, in their establishment outside Sweden are careful to keep the Swedish image in the use of the Swedish letters å, ä and ö as much as possible in the names of furniture. This, of course, was not part of their image inside Sweden. Moreover, they turn to other customers. Outside Sweden their customers are often professionals, whereas in Sweden customers from the start were typically working class or lower middle class. Some transnational organizational concepts have had a remarkable ability to penetrate into different constellations and cultures, although, to avoid pitfalls, they have to pay attention to certain cultural features. The editors of the IKEA catalogue carefully avoid having dogs in pictures in the catalogue, since this could upset potential customers in Bahrein or Saudi Arabia.

For most voluntary associations, at least for social influence associations, much of their activity is concentrated on growing through recruiting new members and followers. For voluntary associations there is a more direct relationship between message, promotion, semi-organized fields and the recruitment of members. Sympathizers often turn into affiliates, whereas customers are rarely made into employees of business enterprises. In the activities of voluntary associations there is a close connection between the work of changing people's values and attitudes and the process of organizing. This has been typical of the Christian mission from its early days until today. Harrison White discusses the interplay between doctrine and relations between followers in the Pauline mission, which led to 'attempts by organizational entrepreneurs to contrive further explicit social pattern, what we call formal organization. The early church was the result' (1992: 106). And Christianity has normally been spread 'through the planting of congregations, which are local groups that evolved into what we call churches' (1992: 107). This spread has been dispersed into competition between several church organizations. Of course, today the largest transnational church organization is the Roman Catholic church, which coordinates activities of almost a billion people within a great number of constellations of organizations.

It is exceptional that states expand their territory through purchase as when the United States bought Alaska from Russia. The enlargement of states usually happens through wars and conquests. Although this is not a spread of the state it implies changing relations of dependence within many organizational constellations. Conquests are often legitimated by the fact that a conqueror has been asked to assist or liberate some group of people within the state under attack, and occupiers often try to install a government led by local people. The colonization of parts of Africa and Asia by European states in the nineteenth century was a massive enforced spread of the state. In the colonies the state organization established new forms of dependencies that were disastrous for many existing forms of organization (see Hydén, 1985: 253–4).

Most of the enlargement of state organizations takes place inside their territories, however. The enlargement of states in this way implies that more human actions take place inside state organizations. Children spend more time in schools and an increasing number of people become state employees.

The spread of organizations is a matter of actions on behalf of organizations. Missionaries, agitators, soldiers and salesmen act with resources and ideas from an organization, and their actions are planned and controlled. For the missionary or the salesman the spread of the message and the activity is routine. They have said and done the same things before, but for the people who encounter these activities for the first time it may be exciting or upsetting, and it may change their lives.

## Institutional diffusion

By institutional diffusion we mean that forms of organization are spread not by an organization itself, but by someone who has learnt a way of organizing that he or she tries to establish in a new place, not as an extension of an existing organization but as a new organization. Often such entrepreneurs are not strangers to the place where they act; only the organizational form is new. This implies a somewhat different causal story. In such a case a new organization is brought to a place from someone inside the constellation.

Often this form of diffusion of organizational forms has been the result of people migrating between regions within a country or between countries. Freemasonry was brought to Holland and France by merchants, and later to North America by immigrants. The first person to agitate for a social-democratic party in Sweden did this after his return from many years in Germany and Denmark. Initially Australian trade unions followed the pattern of British unionism brought there by immigrant craftsmen (Brown, 1983: 252–3). The Hungarian trade union movement developed under German and Austrian influence mainly through immigrant workers (see Erényi, 1977: 18, 21). The International Order of Good Templars, which was founded in the United States in 1851, was brought to Sweden by a Swede returning after seven years in the United States (see Thörnberg, 1938: 100). Soccer as an organized game originated in England and was brought to several countries by visiting English sailors, British embassy personnel or British workers. It was also brought back home by students after the completion of their education in England (see Markovits, 1988: 134). In Sweden soccer was also introduced by Scottish guest workers.

In such cases of diffusion of organizations relations of interdependence between old and new organizations are not as strong and obvious as in the growth of one single organizational body. Yet, there is a dependence on new ideas and there is often an exchange between these organizations, even though they are formally independent of each other.

Even if such organizations are formally separate bodies they may be connected through what we have called organizations of organizations, such as the International Labour Organization or FIFA, the International football federation. Probably the best known organization of organizations is the United Nations.

We believe it is important to distinguish between organizations with individual affiliates and organizations where the 'members' are other organizations. Positions, power, authority and coordination in such organizations of organizations are different from what goes on inside ordinary organizations. Organizations of organizations are particularly important for understanding the promotion of institutional processes. They set standards for rules, forms and activities of their member organizations. They can also be actively involved in establishing new organizations. In this way resources are transferred into new constellations of organizations, which may change relations of power and enable newly established organizations, for instance, a church or a trade union, to survive despite resistance.

Organizations of organizations do not necessarily have to be international. There are also national organizations of organizations such as the British TUC (Trades Union Congress), and national employers' organizations or trade associations.

The expansion of state organizations and activities has to a large extent been affected by institutional and isomorphic processes. Ideas and demands on the state have been carried forward by political parties, unions and professional groups. Many of these ideas have originated in other states or parties, although the particular form of a state agency is contingent on relations of power and time sequences within each constellation of organizational actors. Social insurance is considered a German invention. It was swiftly adapted into Sweden in 1884 (see Olsson, 1990: 40–4), although there were also substantial deviances from the original German legislation, due to different time sequences in different countries (see Kuhnle, 1979). John Meyer (1987a: 50) argues that the rules defining the legitimacy of a state 'are clearly located and shared outside the boundaries of any given nation-state'. The fundamental issues of such rules concern territory, population and means of violence. Such rules are enforced by other states through, for example, economic aid, or arms, and they are also upheld by organizations of organizations such as the United Nations or the World Bank. The importance of external support is particularly obvious in 'peripheral states', which Thomas and Meyer (1987: 109) regard as exogenous constructions. Such strong external support may lead to a loose coupling within the state between formal rules and practices (Meyer, 1987a: 58). In an investigation of the development of state authority and citizens' rights in a large number of states, indicators of the form of the state did not closely follow any internal dynamic, nor did they follow the place of states in international trade. State forms seem to be more similar than they would have been if they had developed mainly out of internal dynamics, which indicates that state forms are also caused by diffusion of universal institutional processes (see Boli, 1987).

Various forms of enterprises are spread through entrepreneurs often in competiton with and against the resistance of existing enterprises. As in the case of voluntary associations, the spread of business has often been accomplished by immigrants. In Sweden many of the first industrial enterprises were founded by Scottish merchants, who came to Sweden for trade during the Napoleonic wars (Therborn, 1989: 90–1).

## Moving organizations

Strictly speaking, only two types of organization are able to move, namely business enterprises and families. States and voluntary associations cannot, or at least do not, move their activities; they can grow and spread, but not move. But both business enterprises and families can and do move their activities from one place to another from one constellation to another, also across considerable geographical distances.

Enterprises often move their production to areas of the social landscape where they can find the most suitable supply of labour power in terms of skills or wage requirements etc. Enterprises may also move away from demands from a certain state in the form of taxes or regulations into other states, or move away from trade unions. That enterprises have the possibility to move and to choose their location can often give them advantages in negotiations with state authorities, although there are many limitations on where and when enterprises are able to move. But particularly in sectors of manufacturing industry where technological change is frequent, possibilities to move increase, and thus the bargaining power of states towards transnational corporations is weakened (Dicken, 1992: 411–12).

Families often have to move within or between countries, and often from the countryside in one country to cities in another country to find their livelihood. In many cases only one or a couple of family members move first to find employment, and the rest of the family comes later. Family members may also live separated for many years and still keep together. In this way families penetrate into new constellations of organizations looking for empty places or niches. The spread of Chinese families is one of the more remarkable cases. Chinese workers were actively recruited to the United States in the late nineteenth century by mining and railway companies (Wong, 1982: 3). Later, whole families moved into the United States. The Chinese rural form of family was well suited for a certain adaptation in the United States, particularly in the form of family businesses, most typically in the Chinese restaurant. Its kinship structure makes for a flexible and strong organization, where authority relations and trust are already established (Wong, 1982: 46–7). The new constellation does not imply a change in the form of the family; on the contrary, it is the old form that makes the establishment in a new constellation and the finding of a niche possible. Chinese families have been able to move, not in spite of but because of the traditional family form.

In other cases traditional kinship structures have been even more reinforced due to changes in constellations. After they were exiled in 1948 many Palestinian families have grown in importance as the source of resources for family members. Several families have developed new organizational forms to cope with the experience as transnational organizations. Family members were dispersed into several continents, but some of the families have established family centres in a house owned or rented by the family, where they have gatherings and celebrate marriages. Some centres distribute newsletters providing information on deaths, births and educational attainments of family members. They have also created family funds to use for the care of sick family members, or for the education of children (Ghabra, 1987: 105–10).

## Reception and resistance

The spread of organizations is far from automatic. It is a struggle that happens between organizations involving competition, conflict and negotiations, and it is enacted through individuals acting on behalf of organizations. The ability to grow, spread and move is to a large extent due to the strength and power of each organization, but what gives power in one constellation of organizations may be fairly useless in another. The spread of an organization is often resisted. Roman Catholic missionaries were successful in Latin America, but they were thrown out of Japan. Donald Roy has investigated resistance of enterprises to trade unions in the southern United States. He distinguished between three resistive tactics: fear stuff, sweet stuff and evil stuff. Fear stuff includes threats of discharges of employees or threats of closing or moving a plant. Sweet stuff may be dispensed as promises or hints of favours such as promotion or improvements in working conditions. Evil stuff implies giving a threatening image of what unions are all about, such as 'wicked intentions, sinister connections, violence and corruption' (Roy, 1980: 409).

On the other hand, the spread of some organizations may achieve an unexpected success in a new constellation of organizations, and an organization may grow faster in a new constellation than in its constellation of origin. The development of the social-democratic party in Russia into a ruling communist party is one example, the survival and spread of Freemasonry in North America is another, and the spread of soccer in countries such as Brazil or Argentina may be a third example.

In the analysis of the diffusion of innovations it is customary to talk about reception of innovations as a process that happens in phases. There is a first slow phase, but when an innovation becomes better known among people, the pressure to adopt or reject it becomes stronger. When adoption has reached a certain threshold 'adoption is more likely to occur as the self-generated network pressures toward adoption increase' (Rogers, 1983: 235). You can also talk about a 'critical mass' or a 'critical number', which makes a process of adoption self-sustaining (Schelling, 1978: 94–5). This seems to be a reasonable argument in many cases, but it probably fits the diffusion of technological devices or products better than organizations. And it is a larger step to change organizational affiliation than to buy a new product.

The spread of organizations is not only governed by people's choices, it is to a large extent determined by resistance or support from other organizations. And the resistance from other organizations may increase when a new organization in a constellation has attracted a critical mass. Established political parties do not attack a new party until it has become a threat.

The timing of organizational spread determines what kind of resistance a new organization will encounter. Possibilities of growth and spread vary with business cycles, which are results of changing relations between organizations. The spread of capitalist enterprises is not a uniform process, and it follows different paths in different constellations of organizations. Relations between a state and growing enterprises have been vastly different in different organizational constellations. Relations between enterprises also vary with the constellation. The growth of capitalism in Great Britain and the United States was much more competitive than in Japan and Germany, for instance (see Orrú, 1993).

New organizations have to find or create an opening in the social landscape. If certain activities are already organized in one form there may not be much room for a new organization. This phenomenon has been called 'crowding out'. The fact that soccer never became a big sport in the United States or Canada has been explained in this way. In the middle of the nineteenth century football was played with different rather fluid rules in public schools and colleges both in England and in the United States. And football was organized and codified in both countries during the 1860s, but with different rules. Since the origin of organized football in the United States and in England happened rather spontaneously at the same time none of these new forms of football could be spread into the other country. When the English model for organized soccer started to spread around the world, its potential space in the United States was already occupied (see Markovits, 1988).

It is also possible to understand the comparative strength of women's organizations in North America compared to Scandinavian countries in this way. In Sweden most women's organizations are branches of political parties. This means that party politics has already occupied at least part of the activities of potential members of women's organizations making the organizational space smaller for an independent women's organization (see Katzenstein, 1987: 5, 10–12). Crowding out can also be actively used to resist new organizations. The Roman Catholic Church, for instance, has been rather successful in setting up trade unions to diminish the room for independent or socialist unions.

It is not altogether clear, however, what constitutes an empty space that can be exploited for organizational endeavours. The meaning of 'empty' depends on the type of activity that is involved. And some organizations may use violence and coercion to make room for themselves. Market research is a method of discovering empty spaces. It is in the logic of capitalist enterprises to produce new needs and to discover new use values (see Marx, 1973: 408).

The opportunities for organizations to grow and spread are finally dependent on people's choices and people's resistance. And people join organizations in order to fight other organizations. Such choices, however, are often affected by organizational promotion of ideologies and ideas.

Organizations are only indirectly influenced by the wishes and goals of individual affiliates. In many organizations people's dreams, visions and hopes are filtered away in decision processes and coordination of actions. And in social processes what is left of visions inside organizations is crushed in the struggle with other organizations.

# REFERENCES

Abrahamsson, Bengt (1993) *The Logic of Organizations*. London: Sage.

Adamson, Nancy, Briskin, Linda and McPhail, Margaret (1988) *Feminist Organizing for Change: The Contemporary Women's Movement in Canada*. Toronto: Oxford University Press.

Adler, Nancy (1991) *International Dimensions of Organizational Behavior*. 2nd edn. Boston, MA: PWS-Kent Publishing.

Ahrne, Göran (1990) *Agency and Organization: Towards an Organizational Theory of Society*. London: Sage.

Aldrich, Howard (1979) *Organizations and Environments*. Englewood Cliffs, NJ: Prentice-Hall.

Aldrich, Howard (1986) 'A population perspective on organizational strategy' in Howard Aldrich, *Population Perspectives on Organizations*. Stockholm: Almqvist & Wiksell International.

Aldrich, Howard (1990) 'Using an ecological perspective to study organizational founding rates', *Entrepreneurship, Theory and Practice*, 14(3): 7–24.

Aldrich, Howard (1992) 'Incommensurable paradigms? Vital signs from three perspectives' in Michael Reed and Michael Hughes (eds), *Rethinking Organizations: New Directions in Organization Theory and Analysis*. London: Sage.

Aldrich, Howard and Mueller, Susan (1982) 'The evolution of organizational forms: technology, coordination and control' in Barry Staw and L.L. Cummings (eds), *Research in Organizational Behaviour*. Volume 4. Greenwich, CT: JAI Press.

Alexander, Jeffrey (1988) 'Sociological theory today' in Neil Smelser (ed.), *Handbook of Sociology*. Beverly Hills, CA: Sage.

Alvesson, Mats (1990) 'Organization: from substance to image', *Organization Studies*, 11(3): 373–94.

Anderson, Benedict (1983) *Imagined Communities: Reflections on the Origin and Spread of Nationalism*. London: Verso.

Archer, Margaret (1990) 'Theory, culture and post-industrial society' in Mike Featherstone (ed.), *Global Culture: Nationalism, Globalization and Modernity*. London: Sage.

Arnason, Johann, P. (1990) 'Nationalism, globalization and modernity' in Mike Featherstone (ed.), *Global Culture: Nationalism, Globalization and Modernity*. London: Sage.

Astley, W. Graham (1985) 'The two ecologies: population and community perspectives on organizational evolution', *Administrative Science Quarterly*, 30(2): 224–41.

Axelrod, Robert (1984) *The Evolution of Cooperation*. New York: Basic Books.

Axelsson, Björn (1992) 'Corporate strategy models and networks – diverging perspectives' in Björn Axelsson and Geoffrey Easton (eds), *Industrial Networks: A New View of Reality*. London: Routledge.

Axelsson, Björn and Johansson, Jan (1992) 'Foreign market entry – the textbook vs. the network view' in Björn Axelsson and Geoffrey Easton (eds), *Industrial Networks: A New View of Reality*. London: Routledge.

Bacharach, Samuel B. and Lawler, Edward J. (1980) *Power and Politics in Organizations*. San Francisco: Jossey-Bass Publishers.

Bacharach, Samuel B. and Lawler, Edward J. (1981) *Bargaining: Power, Tactics and Outcomes*. San Francisco: Jossey-Bass Publishers.

Barbalet, J.M. (1985) 'Power and resistance', *British Journal of Sociology*, 36(4): 531–48.

Barnard, Chester (1968). *The Functions of the Executive*. Thirtieth Anniversary Edition. Cambridge, MA: Harvard University Press.

Baron, James N. (1984) 'Organizational perspectives on stratification', *Annual Review of Sociology*, 10: 37–69.

Baron, James N. and Bielby, William T. (1986) 'The proliferation of job titles in organizations', *Administrative Science Quarterly*, 31(4): 561–86.

Berger, Peter and Luckmann, Thomas (1967) *The Social Construction of Reality*. New York: Anchor Books.

Bhaskar, Roy (1989) 'On the possibility of social scientific knowledge and the limits of naturalism' in Roy Bhaskar, *Reclaiming Reality: A Critical Introduction to Contemporary Philosophy*. London: Verso.

Blauner, Robert (1964) *Alienation and Freedom*. Chicago: University of Chicago Press.

Blom, Raimo, Kivinen, Markku, Melin, Harri and Rantalaiho, Liisa (1992) *The Scope Logic Approach to Class Analysis*. Aldershot: Avebury.

Boli, John (1987) 'World polity sources of expanding state authority and organization, 1870–1970' in George M. Thomas, John W. Meyer, Francisco O. Ramirez and John Boli (eds), *Institutional Structure: Constituting State, Society and the Individual*. Newbury Park, CA: Sage.

Bourdieu, Pierre (1984) *Distinction: A Social Critique of the Judgement of Taste*. London: Routledge & Kegan Paul.

Braudel, Fernand (1982) *The Wheels of Commerce*. London: William Collins.

Brown, Henry Phelps (1983) *The Origins of Trade Union Power*. Oxford: Clarendon Press.

Brown, Rupert (1988) *Group Processes: Dynamics within and between Groups*. Oxford: Basil Blackwell.

Brubaker, Rogers (1992) *Citizenship and Nationhood in France and Germany*. Cambridge, MA: Harvard University Press.

Brunsson, Nils (1985) *The Irrational Organization: Irrationality as a Basis for Organizational Action and Change*. Chichester: John Wiley.

Buckley, Walter (1967) *Sociology and Modern Systems Theory*. Englewood Cliffs, NJ: Prentice-Hall.

Burawoy, Michael (1979) *Manufacturing Consent*. Chicago: University of Chicago Press.

Burawoy, Michael (1985) *The Politics of Production*. London: Verso.

Burns, Tom (1992) *Erving Goffman*. London: Routledge.

Burns, Tom and Stalker, G.M. (1961) *The Management of Innovation*. London: Tavistock Publications.

Castles, Francis G. and Mitchell, Deborah (1992) 'Identifying welfare state regimes: the links between politics, instruments and outcomes', *Governance: An International Journal of Policy and Administration*, 5(1): 1–26.

Chandler, Alfred D. (1977) *The Visible Hand: The Managerial Revolution in American Business*. Cambridge, MA: Belknap Press of Harvard University Press.

Clegg, Stewart R. (1989) *Frameworks of Power*. London: Sage.

Clegg, Stewart R. (1990) *Modern Organizations: Organization Studies in the Postmodern World*. London: Sage.

Cockburn, Cynthia (1991) *In the Way of Women: Men's Resistance to Sex Equality in Organizations*. London: Macmillan.

Cohen, Michael D., March, James G. and Olsen, Johan P. (1982) 'People, problems, solutions and the ambiguity of relevance' in James G. March and Johan P. Olsen (eds), *Ambiguity and Choice in Organizations*. Bergen: Universitetsforlaget.

Coleman, James S. (1990) *Foundations of Social Theory*. Cambridge, MA: Belknap Press of Harvard University Press.

Collins, Randall (1986) *Weberian Sociological Theory*. Cambridge: Cambridge University Press.

Collins, Randall and Coltrane, Scott (1991) *Sociology of Marriage and the Family: Gender, Love and Property*. 3rd edn. Chicago: Nelson-Hall Publishers.

Cooley, Charles Horton (1914) *Social Organization: A Study of the Larger Mind*. New York: Charles Scribner's Sons.

Coser, Lewis A. (1964) 'The political function of eunuchism', *American Sociological Review*, 29(6): 880–5.

Coser, Lewis A. (1967) 'Greedy Organizations', *Archives Européennes de Sociologie*, 7(2): 196–215.

Crozier, Michel (1964) *The Bureaucratic Phenomenon*. Chicago: University of Chicago Press.

Cyert, Richard M. and March, James G. (1963) *A Behavioral Theory of the Firm*. Englewood Cliffs, NJ: Prentice-Hall.

Dalton, Russell J., Kuechler, Manfred and Burklin, Wilhelm (1990) 'The challenge of new movements' in Russell J. Dalton and Manfred Kuechler (eds), *Challenging the Political Order: New Social and Political Movements in Western Democracies*. Cambridge: Polity Press.

Davidson, Donald (1980) 'Causal relations' in Donald Davidson, *Essays on Actions and Events*. Oxford: Oxford University Press.

Dicken, Peter (1992) *Global Shift: The Internationalization of Economic Activity*. 2nd edn. London: Paul Chapman Publishing.

DiMaggio, Paul J.(1991) 'The micro-macro dilemma in organizational research: implications of role-system theory' in Joan Huber (ed.), *Macro–Micro Linkages in Sociology*. Newbury Park, CA: Sage.

DiMaggio, Paul J. and Powell, Walter W. (1991a) 'Introduction' in Walter W. Powell and Paul J. DiMaggio (eds), *The New Institutionalism in Organizational Analysis*. Chicago: University of Chicago Press.

DiMaggio, Paul J. and Powell, Walter W. (1991b) 'The iron cage revisited: institutional isomorphism and collective rationality in organizational fields' in Walter W. Powell and Paul J. DiMaggio (eds), *The New Institutionalism in Organizational Analysis*. Chicago: University of Chicago Press.

Dore, Ronald (1973) *British Factory – Japanese Factory: The Origins of National Diversity in Industrial Relations*. Berkeley: University of California Press.

Edwards, Richard (1979) *Contested Terrain: The Transformation of the Workplace in the Twentieth Century*. New York: Basic Books.

Eisenhardt, Kathleen (1989) 'Agency theory: an assessment and review', *Academy of Management Review*, 14(1): 57–74.

Elias, Norbert (1978) *What is Sociology?* London: Hutchinson.

Elster, Jon (1983) *Explaining Technical Change: A Case Study in the Philosophy of Science*. Cambridge: Cambridge University Press.

Elster, Jon (1989) *The Cement of Society: A Study of Social Order*. Cambridge: Cambridge University Press.

Elster, Jon (1992) 'Argumenter og forhandlinger: om strategisk bruk av kommunikativ atferd', *Tidskrift for Samfunnsforskning*, 33(2): 115–32.

Emerson, Richard M. (1962) 'Power-dependence relations', *American Sociological Review*, 27(1): 31–41.

Erényi, Tibor (1977) 'The origins of the Hungarian trade-union movement' in E. Kabos and A. Zsilák (eds), *Studies on the History of the Hungarian Trade-Union Movement*. Budapest: Akadémiai Kiadó.

Eriksson, Kjell, E. (1991) *Jag slutar: Individuell konfliktlösning i arbetslivet*. Lund: Bokbox.

Esping-Andersen, Gøsta (1990) *The Three Worlds of Welfare Capitalism*. Cambridge: Polity Press.

Etzioni, Amitai (1961) *A Comparative Analysis of Complex Organizations*. New York: Free Press of Glencoe.

Etzioni, Amitai (1968) *The Active Society: A Theory of Societal and Political Processes*. New York: Free Press.

Featherstone, Mike (1991) *Consumer Culture and Postmodernism*. Sage: London.

Fischer, Claude S. (1982) *To Dwell among Friends: Personal Networks in Town and City*. Chicago: University of Chicago Press.

Fligstein, Neil (1985) 'The spread of the multidivisional form among large firms, 1919–1979', *American Sociological Review*, 50(3): 377–91.

Fligstein, Neil (1991) 'The structural transformation of American industry: an institutional account of the causes of diversification in the largest firms, 1919–1979' in Walter W. Powell and Paul J. DiMaggio (eds), *The New Institutionalism in Organizational Analysis*. Chicago: University of Chicago Press.

Fligstein, Neil and Brantley, Peter (1992) 'Bank control, owner control, or organizational dynamics: who controls the large modern corporation?', *American Journal of Sociology*, 98(2): 280–307.

Foucault, Michel (1975) *Discipline and Punish: The Birth of the Prison*. Harmondsworth: Penguin Books.

Friedland, Roger and Alford, Robert R. (1991) 'Bringing society back in: symbols, practices, and institutional contradictions' in Walter W. Powell and Paul J. DiMaggio (eds), *The New Institutionalism in Organizational Analysis*. Chicago: University of Chicago Press.

Fulcher, James (1991) *Labour Movements, Employers, and the State: Conflict and Co-operation in Britain and Sweden*. Oxford: Clarendon Press.

Gamson, William A. (1987) 'Introduction' in Mayer N. Zald and John D. McCarthy (eds), *Social Movements in an Organizational Society*. New Brunswick: Transaction Books.

Garrett, Stephanie (1989) 'Friendship and the social order' in Roy Porter and Sylvana Tomaselli (eds), *The Dialectics of Friendship*. London: Routledge.

Gerth, Hans and Mills, C. Wright (1970) *Character and Social Structure: The Psychology of Social Institutions*. London: Routledge & Kegan Paul.

Ghabra, Shafeeq N. (1987) *Palestinians in Kuwait: The Family and the Politics of Survival*. Boulder, CO: Westview Press.

Giddens, Anthony (1984) *The Constitution of Society*. Cambridge: Polity Press.

Giddens, Anthony (1990a) *Consequences of Modernity*. Cambridge: Polity Press.

Giddens, Anthony (1990b) 'Structuration theory and sociological analysis' in Jon Clark, Celia Modgil and Sohan Modgil (eds), *Anthony Giddens: Consensus and Controversy*. London: The Falmer Press.

Goffman, Erving (1959) *The Presentation of Self in Everyday Life*. Garden City, NY: Doubleday Anchor Books.

Goffman, Erving (1968) *Asylums: Essays on the Social Situation of Mental Patients and Other Inmates*. Harmondsworth: Penguin Books.

Goffman, Erving (1971) *Relations in Public: Microstudies of the Public Order*. New York: Harper & Row.

Goffman, Erving (1972) *Encounters: Two Studies in the Sociology of Interaction*. Harmondsworth: Penguin Books.

Granovetter, Mark S. (1973) 'The strength of weak ties', *American Journal of Sociology*, 78(6): 1360–80.

Granovetter, Mark S. (1985) 'Economic action and social structure: the problem of embeddedness', *American Journal of Sociology*, 91(3): 481–510.

Granovetter, Mark S. (1992) 'Economic institutions as social constructions: a framework for analysis', *Acta Sociologica*, 35(1): 3–11.

Gyllenhammar, Pehr G. (1991) *Även med känsla*. Stockholm: Månpocket.

Hamilton, Gary G. and Biggart, Nicole Woolsey (1992) 'Market, culture and authority: a comparative analysis of management and organization in the far east' in Mark Granovetter and Richard Swedberg (eds), *The Sociology of Economic Life*. Boulder, CO: Westview Press.

Hannan, Michael T. and Freeman, John (1989) *Organizational Ecology*. Cambridge, MA: Harvard University Press.

Hardin, Russell (1982) *Collective Action*. Baltimore, MD: Johns Hopkins University Press.

Harris, Christopher C. (1990) *Kinship*. Milton Keynes: Open University Press.

Hechter, Michael (1987) *Principles of Group Solidarity*. Berkeley: University of California Press.

Heckscher, Charles C. (1993) 'Searching for mutual gains in labor relations' in Lavinia Hall (ed.), *Negotiation: Strategies for Mutual Gain*. Newbury Park, CA: Sage.

Heller, Frank, Drenth, Pieter, Koopman, Paul and Rus, Veljko (1988) *Decisions in Organizations: A Three-Country Comparative Study*. London: Sage.

Herriot, Peter (1992) *The Career Management Challenge. Balancing Individual and Organizational Needs* London: Sage.

Heydebrand, Wolf (1989) 'New organizational forms', *Work and Occupations*, 16(3): 323–57.

Hickson, D.J., Hinnings, C.R., Lee, C.A., Schneck, R.E. and Pennings, J.M. (1971) 'A strategic contingencies' theory of intraorganizational power', *Administrative Science Quarterly*, 16(2): 216–29.

Hintze, Olle (1988) *Fackliga förhandlingar*. Stockholm: Byggförlaget.

Hirschman, Albert (1970) *Exit, Voice and Loyalty: Responses to Decline in Firms, Organizations and States*. Cambridge, MA: Harvard University Press.

Hirschman, Albert (1981) *Essays in Trespassing: Economics to Politics and Beyond*. Cambridge: Cambridge University Press.

Hobson, Barbara (1990) 'No exit, no voice: women's economic dependency and the welfare state', *Acta Sociologica*, 33(3): 235–50.

Hofstede, Geert (1991) *Cultures and Organizations: Software of the Mind*. London: McGraw-Hill.

Hopkins, Terence K. (1982) 'The study of the capitalist world economy: some introductory considerations' in Terence K. Hopkins and Immanuel Wallerstein, *World-Systems Analysis: Theory and Methodology*. Beverly Hills, CA: Sage.

Hydén, Göran (1985) *Utveckling utan genvägar*. Stockholm: Wahlström och Widstrand.

Hydén, Margareta (1992) *Women Battering as Marital Act: The*

*Construction of a Violent Marriage*. Stockholm Studies in Social Work 7. Stockholm: School of Social Work.

Höllinger, Franz and Haller, Max (1990) 'Kinship and social networks in modern societies: a cross-cultural comparison among seven nations', *European Sociological Review*, 6(2): 103–21.

Jacob, Margaret C. (1991) *Living the Enlightenment: Freemasonry and Politics in Eighteenth-Century Europe*. Oxford: Oxford University Press.

Jepperson, Ronald L. (1991) 'Institutions, institutional effects, and institutionalism' in Walter W. Powell and Paul DiMaggio (eds), *The New Institutionalism in Organizational Analysis*. Chicago: University of Chicago Press.

Jepperson, Ronald L. and Meyer, John W. (1991) 'The public order and the construction of formal organizations' in Walter W. Powell and Paul DiMaggio (eds), *The New Institutionalism in Organizational Analysis*. Chicago: University of Chicago Press.

Johansson, Göran (1992) *More Blessed to Give. A Pentecostal Mission to Bolivia in Anthropological Perspective*. Stockholm: Stockholm Studies in Social Anthropology.

Johansson, Roine (1992) *Vid byråkratins gränser*. Lund: Arkiv förlag.

Kangas, Olli (1991) *The Politics of Social Rights. Studies on the Dimensions of Sickness Insurance in OECD Countries*. Stockholm: Swedish Institute for Social Research.

Kanter, Rosabeth Moss (1977) *Men and Women of the Corporation*. New York: Basic Books.

Kapur, Promilla (1973) *Love, Marriage and Sex*. Delhi: Vikas Publishing House.

Katzenstein, Mary Fainsod (1987) 'Comparing the feminist movements of the United States and Western Europe: an overview' in Mary Fainsod Katzenstein and Carol McClurg Mueller (eds), *The Women's Movements of the United States and Western Europe: Consciousness, Political Opportunity, and Public Policy*. Philadelphia: Temple University Press.

Keeley, Michael (1988) *A Social-Contract Theory of Organizations*. Notre Dame, IN: University of Notre Dame Press.

Keesing, Roger M. (1975) *Kin Groups and Social Structure*. Fort Worth: Holt, Rinehart & Winston.

Kerr, Clark, Dunlop, John T., Harbison, Frederick H. and Myers, Charles A. (1960) *Industrialism and Industrial Man: The Problems of Labor and Management in Economic Growth.* Cambridge, MA: Harvard University Press.

Klandermans, P. Bert (1990) 'Linking the "old" and the "new": movement networks in the Netherlands' in Russell J. Dalton and Manfred Kuechler (eds), *Challenging the Political Order: New Social and Political Movements in Western Democracies.* Cambridge: Polity Press.

Klandermans, Bert and Tarrow, Sidney (1988) 'Mobilization into social movements: synthesizing European and American approaches' in Bert Klandermans, Hanspeter Kriesi and Sidney Tarrow (eds), *From Structure to Action: Comparing Social Movement Research across Cultures.* International Social Movement Research. A Research Annual. Volume 1. London: JAI Press.

Knoke, David (1986) 'Associations and interest groups', *Annual Review of Sociology,* 12: 1–21.

Knoke, David (1988) 'Incentives in collective action organizations', *American Sociological Review,* 53(3): 311–29.

Knoke, David and Kuklinski, James H. (1982) *Network Analysis.* Newbury Park, CA: Sage.

Knoke, David and Prensky, David (1984) 'What relevance do organization theories have for voluntary associations?', *Social Science Quarterly,* 65(1): 3–20.

Korpi, Walter (1985) 'Power resources approach vs. action and conflict: on causal and intentional explanation in the study of power', *Sociological Theory,* 3(2): 31–45.

Kuechler, Manfred and Dalton, Russell, J. (1990) 'New social movements and the political order: inducing change for long-term stability?' in Russell J. Dalton and Manfred Kuechler (eds), *Challenging the Political Order: New Social and Political Movements in Western Democracies.* Cambridge: Polity Press.

Kuhnle, Stein (1979) 'The beginnings of the Nordic welfare states: similarities and differences', *Acta Sociologica,* 22(Supplement): 9–35.

Landes, David S. (1986) 'What do bosses really do?', *Journal of Economic History,* 46(3): 585–623.

Latour, Bruno (1986) 'The powers of association' in J. Law (ed.),

*Power, Action and Belief: A New Sociology of Knowledge?* London: Routledge & Kegan Paul.

Lawrence, Paul R. and Lorsch, Jay W. (1986) *Organization and Environment: Managing Differentiation and Integration.* Boston, MA: Harvard Business School Press.

Lazear, Edward P. (1991) 'Labor economics and the psychology of organizations', *Journal of Economic Perspectives,* 5(2): 89–110.

Leiulfsrud, Håkon and Woodward, Alison (1987) 'Women at class crossroads: repudiating conventional theories of family class', *Sociology,* 21(3): 393–412.

Lincoln, James R. and Kalleberg, Arne, M. (1990) *Culture, Control and Commitment: A Study of Work Organization and Work Attitudes in the United States and Japan.* Cambridge: Cambridge University Press.

Lindblom, Charles (1977) *Politics and Markets.* New York: Basic Books.

Lipset, Seymour Martin (1983) 'Radicalism or reformism: the sources of working-class politics', *American Political Science Review,* 77(1): 1–18.

Lipset, Seymour M. and Rokkan, Stein (1967) 'Cleavage structures, party systems, and voter alignments: an introduction' in Seymour M. Lipset and Stein Rokkan (eds), *Party Systems and Voter Alignments: Cross-National Perspectives.* New York: Free Press.

Lipsky, Michael (1980) *Street-Level Bureaucracy: Dilemmas of the Individual in Public Services.* New York: Russell Sage Foundation.

Littler, Craig R. (1982) *The Development of the Labour Process in Capitalist Societies.* London: Heinemann Educational Books.

Lukes, Stephen (1974) *Power: A Radical View.* London: Macmillan Press.

Lysgaard, Sverre (1961) *Arbeiderkollektivet.* Oslo: Universitetsforlaget.

Mann, Michael (1986) *The Sources of Social Power.* Volume 1. Cambridge: Cambridge University Press.

March, James G. and Olsen, Johan P. (1982) 'Attention and the ambiguity of self-interest' in James G. March and Johan P. Olsen (eds), *Ambiguity and Choice in Organizations.* Bergen: Universitetsforlaget.

References 167

March, Robert M. (1988) *The Japanese Negotiator*. Tokyo: Kodansha International.
Markovits, Andrei S. (1988) 'The other "American Exceptionalism" – why is there no soccer in the United States?', *Praxis International*, 8(2): 125–50.
Marshall, Gordon (1990) *In Praise of Sociology*. London: Unwin Hyman.
Marshall, Gordon, Newby, Howard, Rose, David and Vogler, Carolyn (1988) *Social Class in Modern Britain*. London: Hutchinson.
Marshall, Thomas H. (1965) *Class, Citizenship and Social Development*. New York: Anchor Books.
Marx, Karl (1973) *Grundrisse: Introduction to the Critique of Political Economy*. Harmondsworth: Penguin Books.
Marx, Karl (1978) *The Poverty of Philosophy*. Moscow: Progress Publishers.
Mattsson, Lars-Gunnar and Johanson, Jan (1992) 'Network positions and strategic action – an analytical framework' in Björn Axelsson and Geoffrey Easton (eds), *Industrial Networks: A New View of Reality*. London: Routledge.
McCarthy, John D. and Zald, Mayer N. (1987a) 'Resource mobilization and social movements: a partial theory' in Mayer N. Zald and John D. McCarthy (eds), *Social Movements in an Organizational Society*. New Brunswick: Transaction Books.
McCarthy, John D. and Zald, Mayer N. (1987b) 'Appendix: the trend of social movements in America: professionalization and resource mobilization' in Mayer N. Zald and John D. McCarthy (eds), *Social Movements in an Organizational Society*. New Brunswick: Transaction Books.
Merton, Robert (1968) 'Bureaucratic structure and personality' in Robert Merton, *Social Theory and Social Structure*. Enlarged edition. New York: Free Press.
Meyer, John W. (1987a) 'The world polity and the authority of the nation-state' in George M. Thomas, John W. Meyer, Francisco O. Ramirez and John Boli (eds), *Institutional Structure: Constituting State, Society and the Individual*. Newbury Park, CA: Sage.
Meyer, John W. (1987b) 'Self and life course: institutionalization and its effects' in George M. Thomas, John W. Meyer,

Francisco O. Ramirez and John Boli (eds), *Institutional Structure: Constituting State, Society and the Individual*. Newbury Park, CA: Sage.

Meyer, John W. and Rowan, Brian (1991) 'Institutionalized organizations: formal structure as myth and ceremony' in Walter W. Powell and Paul J. DiMaggio (eds), *The New Institutionalism in Organizational Analysis*. Chicago: University of Chicago Press.

Meyer, John W., Boli, John and Thomas, George (1987) 'Ontology and rationalization in the western cultural account' in George M. Thomas, John W. Meyer, Francisco O. Ramirez and John Boli (eds), *Institutional Structure: Constituting State, Society and the Individual*. Newbury Park, CA: Sage.

Meyer, Marshall W. (1985) *Limits to Bureaucratic Growth*. Berlin: Walter de Gruyter.

Meyer, Marshall W. and Zucker, Lynn, G. (1989) *Permanently Failing Organizations*. London: Sage.

Michels, Robert (1962) *Political Parties*. New York: Free Press.

Mintzberg, Henry (1979) *The Structuring of Organizations*. Englewood Cliffs, NJ: Prentice-Hall.

Mintzberg, Henry (1983) *Power In and Around Organizations*. Englewood Cliffs, NJ: Prentice-Hall.

Morgan, D.H.J. (1975) *Social Theory and the Family*. London: Routledge & Kegan Paul.

Olsson, Sven E. (1990) *Social Policy and Welfare State in Sweden*. Lund: Arkiv förlag.

Orrú, Marco (1993) 'Institutional cooperation in Japanese and German capitalism' in Sven-Erik Sjöstrand (ed.), *Institutional Change: Theory and Empirical Findings*. Armonk, NY: M.E. Sharpe.

Ouchi, William G. (1977) 'The relationship between organizational structure and organizational control', *Administrative Science Quarterly*, 22(1): 95–113.

Ouchi, William G. and Wilkins, Alan L. (1985) 'Organizational culture', *Annual Review of Sociology*, 11: 457–83.

Outhwaite, William (1987) *New Philosophies of Social Science: Realism, Hermeneutics and Critical Theory*. New York: St Martin's Press.

Pahl, R.E. (1984) *Divisions of Labour*. Oxford: Basil Blackwell.

Parsons, Talcott (1971) *The System of Modern Societies*. Englewood Cliffs, NJ: Prentice-Hall.

Pateman, Carole (1989) 'Feminist critiques of the public/private dichotomy' in Carole Pateman, *The Disorder of Women*. Cambridge: Polity Press.

Perrow, Charles (1978) 'Demystifing organizations' in Rosemary C. Sarri and Yeheskel Hasenfeld (eds), *The Management of Human Services*. New York: Columbia University Press.

Perrow, Charles (1984) *Normal Accidents: Living with High-Risk Technologies*. New York: Basic Books.

Perrow, Charles (1986) *Complex Organizations: A Critical Essay*. 3rd edn. New York: Random House.

Peterson, Tomas (1993) *Den svengelska modellen*. Lund: Arkiv förlag.

Pfeffer, Jeffrey (1981) *Power in Organizations*. Boston, MA: Pitman.

Pfeffer, Jeffrey and Salancik, Gerald R. (1978) *The External Control of Organizations*. New York: Harper & Row.

Pontusson, Jonas (1990) 'The politics of new technology and job redesign: a comparison of Volvo and British Leyland', *Economic and Industrial Democracy*, 11(3): 311–36

Popenoe, David (1988) *Disturbing the Nest: Family Change and Decline in Modern Societies*. New York: Aldine de Gruyter.

Porter, Roy and Tomaselli, Sylvana (eds) (1989) *The Dialectics of Friendship*. London: Routledge.

Poulantzas, Nicos (1978) *State, Power, Socialism*. London: Verso.

Powell, Walter W. (1991) 'Expanding the scope of institutional analysis' in Walter W. Powell and Paul J. DiMaggio (eds), *The New Institutionalism in Organizational Analysis*. Chicago: University of Chicago Press.

Price, James L. (1989) 'The impact of turnover on the organization', *Work and Occupations*, 16(4): 461–73.

Ragin, Charles C. (1987) *The Comparative Method: Moving Beyond Qualitative and Quantitative Strategies*. Berkeley: University of California Press.

Reed, Michael I. (1992) *The Sociology of Organizations: Themes, Perspectives and Prospects*. Hemel Hempstead: Harvester, Wheatsheaf.

Roberts, John (1972) *The Mythology of Secret Societies*. London: Secker & Warburg.

Robertson, D.B. (1966) 'Hobbes's theory of associations in the seventeenth-century milieu' in D.B. Robertson (ed.), *Voluntary Associations: A Study of Groups in Free Society*. Richmond, VA: John Knox Press.

Robertson, Roland (1992) *Globalization: Social Theory and Global Culture*. London: Sage.

Rochon, Thomas R. (1990) 'The West European Peace Movement and the theory of new social movements' in Russell J. Dalton and Manfred Kuechler (eds), *Challenging the Political Order: New Social and Political Movements in Western Democracies*. Cambridge: Polity Press.

Rogers, Everett, M. (1983) *Diffusion of Innovations*. 3rd edn. New York: Free Press.

Rokkan, Stein (1967) 'The structuring of mass politics in the smaller European democracies: a developmental typology', *Comparative Studies in Society and History*, 10(1): 173–210.

Rose, Arnold M. (1954) *Theory and Method in the Social Sciences*. Minneapolis: University of Minnesota Press.

Rosengren, Annette (1991) *Två barn och eget hus*. Stockholm: Carlssons.

Roy, Donald F. (1980) 'Fear stuff, sweet stuff and evil stuff: management's defenses against unionization in the south' in Theo Nichols (ed.), *Capital and Labour: Studies in the Capitalist Labour Process*. Glasgow: William Collins (Fontana Paperback).

Rueschemeyer, Dietrich, Stephens, Evelyne Huber and Stephens, John D. (1992) *Capitalist Development and Democracy*. Cambridge: Polity Press.

Sahlin-Andersson, Kerstin (1990) *Forskningsparker och företagsrelationer*. Stockholm: Regionplane- och Trafikkontoret.

Sandberg, Åke, Broms, Gunnar, Grip, Arne, Sundström, Lars, Steen, Jesper and Ullmark, Peter (1992) *Technological Change and Co-Determination in Sweden*. Philadelphia: Temple University Press.

Sartre, Jean-Paul (1976) *Critique of Dialectical Reason 1: Theory of Practical Ensembles*. London: New Left Books.

Schelling, Thomas C. (1978) *Micromotives and Macrobehavior*. New York: W.W. Norton.

Schutz, Alfred (1962) 'On multiple realities' in Alfred Schutz, *Collected Papers I: The Problem of Social Reality*. Edited by Maurice Natanson. The Hague: Martinus Nijhoff.

Scott, Richard W. (1992) *Organizations: Rational, Natural and Open Systems*. 3rd edn. Englewood Cliffs, NJ: Prentice-Hall.

Scott, Richard W. and Meyer, John W. (1991) 'The organization of societal sectors: propositions and early evidence' in Walter W. Powell and Paul J. Dimaggio (eds), *The New Institutionalism in Organizational Analysis*. Chicago: University of Chicago Press.

Selznick, Philip (1948) 'Foundations of the theory of organization', *American Sociological Review*, 13(1): 25–35.

Sgritta, Giovanni B. (1989) 'Towards a new paradigm: family in the welfare state crisis' in Katja Boh, Maren Bak, Cristine Clason, Maja Pankratova, Jens Qvortrup, Giovanni B. Sgritta and Kari Waerness (eds), *Changing Patterns of European Family Life: A Comparative Analysis of 14 European Countries*. London: Routledge.

Silverman, David (1971) *The Theory of Organizations: A Sociological Framework*. New York: Basic Books.

Simmel, Georg (1964) *Conflict and the Web of Group-Affiliations*. New York: Free Press.

Simon, Herbert A. (1991) 'Organizations and markets', *Journal of Economic Perspectives*, 5(2): 25–44.

Stinchcombe, Arthur L. (1965) 'Social structure and organizations' in James G. March (ed.), *Handbook of Organizations*. Chicago: Rand McNally.

Stinchcombe, Arthur L. (1990) *Information and Organizations*. Berkeley: University of California Press.

Swedberg, Richard (1993) *Markets as Social Structures*. Work – Organization – Economy Working Paper Series No. 7, Department of Sociology, Stockholm University.

Sztompka, Piotr (1991) *Society in Action: The Theory of Social Becoming*. Cambridge: Polity Press.

Tayeb, Monir H. (1988) *Organizations and National Culture: A Comparative Analysis*. London: Sage.

Therborn, Göran (1983) 'Why some classes are more successful than others', *New Left Review*, 138 (March–April): 37–56.

Therborn, Göran (1989) *Borgarklass och byråkrati i Sverige.* Lund: Arkiv förlag.

Thomas, George M. and Meyer, John W. (1987) 'Regime changes and state power in an intensifying world-state-system' in George M. Thomas, John W. Meyer, Francisco O. Ramirez and John Boli (eds), *Institutional Structure: Constituting State, Society and the Individual.* Newbury Park, CA: Sage.

Thompson, James (1967) *Organizations in Action.* New York: McGraw-Hill.

Thörnberg, E.H. (1938) *Sverige i Amerika: Amerika i Sverige.* Stockholm: Albert Bonniers Förlag.

Tiger, Lionel and Sheper, Joseph (1975) *Women in the Kibbutz.* New York: Harcourt Brace Jovanovich.

Tilly, Charles (1990) *Coercion, Capital and European States AD 990–1990.* Cambridge, MA: Basil Blackwell.

Tocqueville, Alexis, de (1961) *Democracy in America.* Volume 2. New York: Schocken Books.

Turner, Jonathan H. (1988) *A Theory of Social Interaction.* Cambridge: Polity Press.

Udéhn, Lars (1993) 'Twenty-five years with *The Logic of Collective Action*', *Acta Sociologica*, 36(3): 239–62.

Urry, John (1990) *The Tourist Gaze: Leisure and Travel in Contemporary Societies.* London: Sage.

Ury, William (1993) *Getting Past No: Negotiating Your Way from Confrontation to Cooperation.* Revised edition. New York: Bantam Books.

Vamplew, Wray (1988) *Pay Up and Play the Game: Professional Sport in Britain 1875–1914.* Cambridge: Cambridge University Press.

Veneziani, Bruno (1986) 'The evolution of the contract of employment' in Bob Hepple (ed.), *The Making of Labour Law in Europe: A Comparative Study of Nine Countries up to 1945.* London: Mansell Publishing.

Verdon, Michel (1981) 'Kinship, marriage and the family: an operational approach', *American Journal of Sociology*, 86(4): 796–818.

Wallerstein, Immanuel (1990) 'Culture as the ideological battleground of the modern world-system' in Mike Featherstone (ed.), *Global Culture: Nationalism, Globalization and Modernity.* London: Sage.

Wallerstein, Immanuel (1991) 'World-systems analysis: the second phase' in Immanuel Wallerstein, *Unthinking Social Science: The Limits of Nineteenth-Century Paradigms.* Cambridge: Polity Press.

Walzer, Michael (1983) *Spheres of Justice: A Defence of Pluralism and Equality.* Oxford: Martin Robertson.

Weber, Max (1968) *Economy and Society.* Volumes 1 and 2. Edited by Guenther Roth and Claus Wittich. Berkeley: University of California Press.

Wellman, Barry (1988) 'Structural analysis: from method and metaphor to theory and substance' in B. Wellman and S.D. Berkowitz (eds), *Social Structures: A Network Approach.* Cambridge: Cambridge University Press.

Wernick, Andrew (1991) *Promotional Culture: Advertising, Ideology and Symbolic Expression.* London: Sage.

White, Harrison C. (1981) 'Where do markets come from?', *American Journal of Sociology,* 87(3): 517–47.

White, Harrison C. (1992) 'Agency as control in formal networks' in Nitin Nohria and Robert G. Eccles (eds), *Networks and Organizations: Structure, Form and Action.* Boston, MA: Harvard Business School Press.

Williamson, Oliver E. (1985) *The Economic Institutions of Capitalism: Firms, Markets, Relational Contracting.* New York: Free Press.

Williamson, Oliver E. (1991) 'Comparative economic organization: the analysis of discrete structural alternatives', *Administrative Science Quarterly,* 36(2): 269–96.

Willmott, Hugh (1990) 'Beyond paradigmatic closure in organizational enquiry' in John Hassard and Denis Pym (eds), *The Theory and Philosophy of Organizations: Critical Issues and New Perspectives.* London: Routledge.

Willmott, Paul (1987) *Friendship, Networks and Social Support.* London: Policy Studies Institute.

Wong, Bernard P. (1982) *Chinatown: Economic Adaptation and Ethnic Identity of the Chinese.* New York: Holt, Rinehart & Winston.

Woodward, Joan (1965) *Industrial Organization: Theory and Practice.* London: Oxford University Press.

Wright, Erik Olin (1985) *Classes*. London: Verso.

Wright, Erik Olin (1989) 'Rethinking once again the concept of class structure' in Erik Olin Wright et al., *The Debate on Classes*. London: Verso.

Zolberg, Aristide, R. (1986) 'How many exceptionalisms?' in Ira Katznelson and Aristide R. Zolberg (eds), *Working-Class Formation: Nineteenth-Century Patterns in Western Europe and the United States*. Princeton, NJ: Princeton University Press.

Zucker, Lynne G. (1983) 'Organizations as institutions' in S.B. Bachrach (ed.), *Research in the Sociology of Organizations*. Greenwich, CT: JAI Press.

Zukin, Sharon (1991) *Landscapes of Power: From Detroit to Disney World*. Berkeley: University of California Press.

# INDEX

Compiled by Jackie McDermott